Teaching
Analysis of Film Language

David Wharton and Jeremy Grant

Series Editor: Vivienne Clark
Commissioning Editor: Wendy Earle

 Education

British Library Cataloguing–in–Publication Data
A catalogue record for this guide is available in the British Library

ISBN 978 0 85170 981 9

First published in 2005 by the British Film Institute
21 Stephen Street, London W1T 1LN

Reprinted 2007

Student worksheets to support this guide are supplied at: www.bfi.org.uk/tfms
User name: **filmlang@bfi.org.uk**   Password: **te1306fl**

Design: Amanda Hawkes
Cover photograph: *Donnie Darko* (Richard Kelly, USA, 2001) – courtesy of *bfi* Stills
Printed in Great Britain by: Cromwell Press Ltd

www.bfi.org.uk

The British Film Institute's purpose is to champion moving image culture
in all its richness and diversity across the UK, for the benefit of as wide
an audience as possible, and to create and encourage debate.

Contents

Introduction to the series

Since the introduction of the revised post-16 qualifications (AS and A2 Level) in the UK in September 2000, the number of students taking A Level Film and Media Studies has increased significantly. For example, the latest entry statistics show the following trend:

Subject & Level	June 2001	June 2002	June 2004
A Level Film Studies†	2,017	—	—
AS Level Film Studies	3,852	—	7,996
A2 Level Film Studies	—	2,175	4,161
A Level Media Studies*†	16,293	—	—
AS Level Media Studies*	22,872	—	30,745
A2 Level Media Studies*	—	18,150	22,746

*Three combined awarding bodies' results
† Legacy syllabi – last entry June 2001
(*bfi* Education website – AS/A2 statistics refer to cashed-in entries only)

In September 2006, a new A Level specification (syllabus), Moving Image Arts (offered by the Northern Ireland awarding body, CCEA), will be available throughout the UK and it is likely to attract even more students to this lively and popular subject area.

Inevitably, increases in student numbers have led to a pressing demand for more teachers. But, given the comparatively recent appearance of both subjects at degree-level (and limited availability of specialist post-graduate teaching courses), both new and experienced teachers from other disciplines are faced with teaching these subjects for the first time, without a degree-level background to help them with subject content and conceptual understanding. In addition, these specifications saw the arrival of new set topics and areas of study, some of which change frequently, so there is a pressing need for up-to-date resources to help teacher preparation, as well as continuing professional development courses.

I meet a large number of Film and Media Studies teachers every year in the course of my various roles and developed the concept and format of this series with the above factors, and busy and enthusiastic teachers, in mind. Each title provides an accessible reference resource, with essential topic content, as well as clear guidance on good classroom practice to improve the quality of teaching and students' learning. We are confident that, as well as supporting the teacher new to these subjects, the series provides the experienced specialist with new critical perspectives and teaching approaches as well as useful content.

The two sample schemes of work included in Section 1 are intended as practical models to help get teachers started. They are not prescriptive, as any effective scheme of work has to be developed with the specific requirements of an assessment context, and ability of the teaching group, in mind. Likewise, the worksheets provided in the online materials offer examples of good practice, which can be adapted to your specific needs and contexts. In some cases, the online resources include additional resources, such as interviews and illustrative material, available as webnotes. See www.bfi.org.uk/tfms.

The series is clear evidence of the range, depth and breadth of teacher expertise and specialist knowledge required at A Level in these subjects. Also, it is an affirmation of why this subject area is such an important, rich and compelling one for increasing numbers of 16- to 19-year-old students. Many of the more theoretical titles in the series include reference to practical exercises involving media production skills. It is important that it is understood here that the current A Levels in Media and Film Studies are not designed as vocational, or pre-vocational, qualifications. In these contexts, the place of practical media production is to offer students active, creative and engaging ways in which to explore theory and reflect on their own practice.

It has been very gratifying to see that the first titles in this series have found an international audience, in the USA, Canada and Australia, among others, and we hope that future titles continue to be of interest in international moving image education.

Every author in the series is an experienced practitioner of Film and/or Media Studies at this level and many have examining/moderating experience. It has been a pleasure to work closely with such a diverse range of committed professionals and I should like to thank them for their individual contributions to this expanding series.

Vivienne Clark
Series Editor
April 2005

● Key features

- Assessment contexts for the major UK post-16 Film and Media Studies specifications
- Suggested schemes of work
- Historical contexts (where appropriate)
- Key facts, statistics and terms
- Detailed reference to the key concepts of Film and Media Studies
- Detailed case studies
- Glossaries
- Bibliographies
- Student worksheets, activities and resources (available online) – ready for you to print and photocopy for the classroom.

● Other titles available in the series include:

Teaching Scriptwriting, Screenplays and Storyboards for Film and TV Production (Mark Readman)
Teaching TV Sitcom (James Baker)
Teaching Digital Video Production (Pete Fraser and Barney Oram)
Teaching TV News (Eileen Lewis)
Teaching Women and Film (Sarah Gilligan)
Teaching World Cinema (Kate Gamm)
Teaching TV Soaps (Lou Alexander and Alison Cousens)
Teaching Contemporary British Broadcasting (Rachel Viney)
Teaching Contemporary British Cinema (Sarah Casey Benyahia)
Teaching Music Video (Pete Fraser)
Teaching Auteur Study (David Wharton and Jeremy Grant)
Teaching Men and Film (Matthew Hall)
Teaching Film Censorship and Controversy (Mark Readman).

● Forthcoming titles include:

Teaching Video Games; *Teaching Stars and Performance*; *Teaching TV Drama*; *Teaching Analysis of Television Language*; *Teaching Short Films*; *Teaching Music and the Moving Image*.

For details of all these titles go to www.bfi.org.uk/tfms

SERIES EDITOR: Vivienne Clark is a former Head of Film and Media Studies and an Advanced Skills Teacher. She is currently an Associate Tutor of *bfi* Education and Principal Examiner for A Level Media Studies for one of the English awarding bodies. She is a freelance teacher trainer, media consultant and writer/editor, with several published textbooks and resources, including *GCSE Media Studies* (Longman 2002), *Key Concepts and Skills for Media*

Studies (Hodder Arnold 2002) and *The Complete A–Z Film and Media Studies Handbook* (Hodder & Stoughton 2006). She is also a course tutor for the *bfi*/Middlesex University MA module, An Introduction to Media Education, and a link tutor for the Central School of Speech & Drama PGCE (Media with English), London.

AUTHORS:

David Wharton has been a teacher since 1991. He was formerly Subject Co-ordinator for Media Studies and is currently Subject Co-ordinator for Film Studies at Gateway Sixth Form College, Leicester. He has delivered workshops in Film Authorship for the *bfi*, and examines AS Level Film Studies for a British awarding body.

Jeremy Grant has taught in Spain, Poland and the UK. He currently works at Gateway Sixth Form College, Leicester, where he has delivered courses in Film, English and Media Studies since 2000. The authors also collaborated on *Teaching Auteur Study* for this series.

Introduction

Assessment contexts

	Awarding body & level	Subject	Unit code	Module/Topic
✓	AQA AS Level	Media Studies	MED1	Reading the Media
✓	AQA AS Level	Media Studies	MED2	Textual Topics in Contemporary Media
✓	AQA A2 Level	Media Studies	MED4	Texts and Contexts
✓	AQA A2 Level	Media Studies	MED6	Comparative Critical Analysis
✓	OCR AS Level	Media Studies	2731	Textual Analysis
✓	OCR A2 Level	Media Studies	2735	Media Issues and Debates
✓	WJEC AS Level	Media Studies	ME1	Modern Media Forms
✓	WJEC A2 Level	Media Studies	ME4	Investigating Media Texts
✓	WJEC A2 Level	Media Studies	ME6	Text and Context
✓	WJEC AS Level	Film Studies	FS1	Making Meaning 1
✓	WJEC AS Level	Film Studies	FS2	Producers and Audiences
✓	WJEC AS Level	Film Studies	FS3	British Cinema: Messages and Values
✓	WJEC A2 Level	Film Studies	FS4	Making Meaning 2
✓	WJEC A2 Level	Film Studies	FS5	Studies in World Cinema
✓	WJEC A2 Level	Film Studies	FS6	Critical Studies
✓	CCEA AS Level	Moving Image Arts	AS 1	Creative Production
✓	CCEA AS Level	Moving Image Arts	AS 2	Critical Response
✓	CCEA AS Level	Moving Image Arts	A2 1	Creative Production and Research Portfolio
✓	CCEA AS Level	Moving Image Arts	A2 2	Critical Response and Specialisation
✓	SQA Higher	Media Studies	DF14 12	Media Analysis (Fiction)
✓	SQA Advanced Higher	Media Studies	Unit 1	Media Analysis

This guide is also relevant to the following specifications, as well as to international and Lifelong Learning courses:

- AQA, Ed-Excel, OCR – GNVQ and AVCE media and communication
- BTEC National Diploma.

The following titles in this series would be useful companions to this guide:

- *Teaching Scriptwriting, Storyboards and Screenplays for Film and TV Production* (Mark Readman)
- *Teaching Digital Video Production* (Pete Fraser and Barney Oram)
- *Teaching World Cinema* (Kate Gamm)
- *Teaching Women and Film* (Sarah Gilligan)
- *Teaching Men and Film* (Matthew Hall)
- *Teaching Auteur Study* (David Wharton and Jeremy Grant)

Also see:

- *Understanding Film Texts: Meaning and Experience* by Patrick Phillips, published by the *bfi*.
- *The Western* by Richard Harvey and Jill Poppy at
  http://www.bfi.org.uk/education/resources/teaching/fms/Western/

For updates on other *bfi* resources which support this topic go to: www.bfi.org.uk/education

In addition to its principal intended use as a guide for A Level teaching and equivalent international courses, this guide will be valuable at undergraduate level, particularly for students who have no previous experience of Film Studies at A2 Level.

Specification links

This title is relevant to all study of film in the current post-16 specifications, including practical media production of students' own film projects, but the following contexts have a special focus on film language and production.

AQA AS and A2 Level Media Studies

- In MED1 Reading the Media, students are required to study all media forms, including film, for an exam on an unseen media text extract. If the extract is from a film, the student would be expected to comment on such aspects as genre, narrative and representation.
- In MED2, Textual Topics in Contemporary Media, students must apply concepts learnt in MED1 to two media topics, including Film and Broadcast Fiction and Documentary, which both require an understanding of film language. Students have to answer two questions with reference to a range of moving image texts.

- In MED4, Texts and Contexts in the Media, students have the option to study genre for one of two questions – Case study 1 is relevant here.
- An understanding of film language is also relevant to the synoptic unit, MED6, Comparative Critical Analysis.

OCR AS and A2 Level Media Studies

- For Unit 2731, Textual Analysis, students are required to write a detailed textual analysis of an unseen sequence from an action adventure film. Case study 3 supports this unit, as does the introduction to the key concepts of microanalysis in Section 2, using *Die Hard: With a Vengeance* (John McTiernan, USA, 1995) as a focus.
- In Unit 2735, Media Issues and Debates, one of the options for Section B is The Concept of Genre in Film. The introduction of key concepts, using *High Noon* (Fred Zinnemann, USA, 1952) as a focus, and Case study 1 on prison movies, in particular, supports this unit.

WJEC AA and A Level Media Studies

- In Unit ME1 of WJEC AS Level Media Studies, Modern Media Forms, students are expected to understand, amongst other things, aspects of film language in preparation for a one a half hour examination.
- The skills learnt in this module are also relevant to Unit ME4, Investigating Media Texts, which focuses on genre, narrative and representation. This is assessed by a coursework essay of 2–3000 words. Film language is also relevant to the synoptic unit ME6, Text and Context. This usually focuses on a specific genre (documentary, for example).

WJEC AS and A2 Level Film Studies

- Analysis of film language is a core element of the Film Studies specification, featuring in all six units to a greater or lesser degree.
- The whole of the Making Meaning unit, FS1, in the AS course is concerned with developing students' grasp of film language.
- The British and World Cinema Units (FS3 and FS5) require exploration of focus films and close study films in terms of their visual and auditory language.
- The Auteur Research Project and the creative elements of the FS1 and FS4 units all depend on students having developed an independent grasp of film language at both the macro and micro levels.
- Many of the synoptic elements of FS6, such as Shocking Cinema, Authorship and Genre, Performance and Feminist Perspectives, have to be approached through the interpretation of film language.

CCEA AS Level Moving Image Arts

At the time of writing, this specification was in pilot form.

- Units AS1 (Creative Production) and AS2 (Critical Response) both require students to demonstrate competence in film language. They must also demonstrate 'familiarity with the production framework'.
- Unit A2 1 (Creative Production and Research Portfolio) requires students to apply a fluent understanding of the forms and conventions of their chosen medium, which may be film. Unit A2 2 (Critical Response and Specialisation) examines candidates on unseen moving image extracts, including film.

SQA Higher Media Studies

- Responses to film in Unit DF14 12, Media Analysis – Fiction, require an understanding of the main elements of film language at macro and micro levels.

SQA Advanced Higher Media Studies

- Unit 1 (Media Analysis) requires in both parts of the examination that students answer questions relating to 'context-centred, text-centred and audience-centred methods of media analysis'. Film language and production provide excellent examples for all three areas.

What is film language?

In his 1948 essay, 'The birth of a new avant-garde: *le caméra-stylo*', the French film critic Alexandre Astruc wrote:

> The cinema is quite simply becoming a means of expression, just as all the arts have been before it, and in particular painting and the novel. After having been successfully a fairground attraction, an amusement analogous to boulevard theatre, or a means of preserving the images of an era, it is gradually becoming a language. By language, I mean a form in which and by which an artist can express his thoughts, however abstract they may be, or translate his obsessions exactly as he does in the contemporary essay or novel. That is why I would like to call this new age of cinema the age of *caméra-stylo* (cited in Caughie, *Theories of Authorship*, 1981, p9).

What Astruc describes as the language of film is the focus of this guide. Whereas he defines it as 'a means of expression', we would add to this definition the following:

- Film language refers to the means by which meaning is created in a film – to tell a story, create a character and so on.

- This includes dialogue and voiceover, but really focuses on cinematic aspects such as cinematography, *mise en scène*, editing, sound and special effects (SFX), as well as genre, narrative, representation and the star system.

- Film language is a system of signs. Audiences use these signs to construct meaning and this is often in relation to other texts. When we see a star on screen, we are probably aware of other films s/he has been in and this will influence our response to the character. This approach to reading a film as a system of signs is called semiotics and is influenced by the writings of the French critical theorist, Roland Barthes.

- Film language is not fixed – it evolves over time. For example, the rules of continuity editing were developed during the Hollywood studio system (1930–1948), but are now an accepted part of Western film grammar. No doubt new developments in technology will allow film language to evolve in different directions, as we shall see from our discussion of SFX in *Donnie Darko* (Richard Kelly, USA, 2001).

- Film language is not universal – it is specific to place. A comparison of Hollywood films with, for example, *Tokyo Story* (Yasujiro Ozu, Japan, 1953) illuminates how different 'Japanese' film language is from that of the West – in particular, the way Ozu uses a low camera position to reproduce the point of view of someone sitting on a tatami mat. To explore the idea of an alternative film language with your class, see **Worksheets 1a & b** and **student notes**.

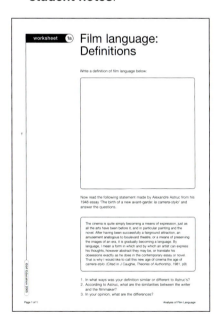

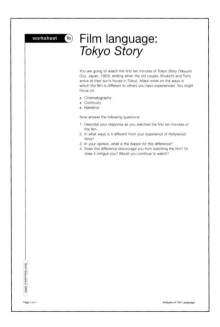

To access worksheets and other online materials go to **www.bfi.org.uk/tfms** and enter User name: **filmlang@bfi.org.uk** and Password: **te1306fl**.

Tokyo Story

In our discussion of film language, we have made a number of distinctions. The main distinction is between macro analysis and microanalysis. We have taken these terms from the WJEC Film Studies specification, but the concepts they describe are relevant to any analysis of film:

- **Macro analysis** focuses primarily on the way film language works within the film as a whole (narrative) or in relation to a group of films (genre), but also includes such aspects as representation and the star system. Macro analysis may be:

  (a) Discussion of a film in relation to a group of films;
  (b) An account of the way a sequence is part of larger patterns within a film, such as the development of character or themes.

- **Micro analysis** refers to analysis of the production techniques used to create meaning in an individual scene – for example, cinematography, *mise en scène*, editing, sound and SFX.

These are rough descriptions. A macro analysis cannot function without making reference to the microelements. How could we consider a film's presentation of a character without considering the way in which that character is lit and photographed? Equally, the production of a micro analysis almost always involves some discussion about the sequence's implications regarding the film's larger structures. For example, when micro analysing a fight sequence, we almost always need to ask, 'who is the hero and who is the villain here?'

It is a mistake to see micro analysis as a purely technical account of a film extract. There are usually clues within a sequence about the larger structures of the film, and it is essential for students producing a micro analysis to write about these. For example, in the extract of *Spider-Man 2* (Sam Raimi, USA, 2004) (Case study 3), it is obvious that the sequence is part of a longer-term romantic development between the characters of Peter and Mary Jane. Much of the technical language of *mise en scène*, camerawork and editing is devoted to this aspect of the narrative.

Micro and macro analyses are distinguished from each other in that one focuses on what is happening immediately before our eyes and ears, while the other is more concerned with the film as a whole. It is a question of emphasis.

Other distinctions we think are useful in our analysis of film language are:

- Studio-produced/independent film: we have tried to demonstrate where possible how the production context of a film influences film language and the meaning it generates;
- Mainstream/arthouse film: we have also tried to show how different audiences construct meaning, or are expected to, in different ways;
- Hollywood/British/World cinema: finally, we think it is important to note how film language is specific to place – see **Worksheets 1a** and **b**, and accompanying **student notes**.

The focus of this guide is on film language, but this is inextricably bound up with production – in other words, the practical process of making a film. This might include anything from writing the screenplay to what happens in the editing room. Traditionally, film production has been divided into three stages:

- Pre-production: for example, writing, storyboarding, casting, set design and costume;
- Production: for example, shooting and performance;
- Post-production: for example, editing, sound and SFX.

We will examine the creation of meaning at all three stages. You can introduce students to the idea of production using **Worksheet 2**.

To access worksheets and other online materials go to **www.bfi.org.uk/tfms** and enter User name: **filmlang@bfi.org.uk** and Password: **te1306fl**.

1 of 2 pages

Getting started

● Why study film language?

Film language is an important area of study in Film and Media Studies for a number of reasons:

- It is a core module, or one of the key concepts, in most A Level Film and Media Studies specifications, but the guide can be used as an introduction to any film course.
- Close textual analysis is required by examiners in most moving image modules. Examiners credit detailed reference to specific textual examples. With this in mind, the study of film language is relevant to all academic aspects of Film Studies.
- More importantly perhaps, an understanding of film language gives students the critical tools they need to analyse films independently.
- A detailed understanding of how meaning is created in a scene also prepares students for their own film productions – increasingly popular on Film and Media Studies courses. It is not only necessary that students understand the basics of continuity, for example, but also that they understand filmmaking as a decision-making process. The focus on film production is obviously important here.

● How to use this guide

We have divided the guide as follows:

- Section 2 introduces the key concepts of film language. Those relating to macro analysis are introduced on pp22–38, with close reference to *High Noon*, and those relating to micro analysis are introduced on pp38–62, with close reference to *Die Hard: With a Vengeance.*
- Section 3 includes three case studies. Firstly, we look at the prison genre as an example of macro analysis. The focus films here are *The Birdman of Alcatraz* (John Frankenheimer, USA, 1962), *The Shawshank Redemption* (Frank Darabont, USA, 1994), *The Magdalene Sisters* (Peter Mullan, UK, 2002). Secondly, we present two examples of micro analysis. The first is of an arthouse film, and the second of a more mainstream Hollywood production. These are, respectively, *Donnie Darko* and *Spider-Man 2*.

If you are new to teaching film language and production, we recommend that you read Section 2 first as this introduces the key concepts and provides various teaching ideas. You could then go onto use one of the case studies in Section 3 as a focus in class.

It is best to obtain copies of the key films listed above (preferably on DVD in order to access the special features) before reading each section, as we will be referring to these texts in some detail. It would also be worthwhile purchasing copies of *Tokyo Story* and *Smoke* (Wayne Wang, USA, 1995) which are referred to in the online resources. Both sections are thoroughly supported with online resources, most of which refer to the focus films listed above. Unless indicated otherwise, the materials in bold text are available at: www.bfi.org.uk/tfms. To access the pages, enter **username**: **filmlang@bfi.org.uk** and **password: te1306fl**. If you have any problems accessing the pages, email: education.resources@bfi.org.uk.

Some of the resources for this guide include stills. In some cases, a black-and-white printout is sufficient, since students will be viewing the film in any case, and the function of the stills is as an *aide memoire.* Others (for example **Worksheet 13** on lighting) should ideally be reproduced in colour. If the cost of doing so is prohibitive, you might photocopy a class set in black and white and reproduce one colour copy on an OHT transparency or electronic whiteboard for classroom use.

On pp16–19 are two examples of schemes of work focusing on macro and micro elements of film language. These are starting points and we anticipate teachers using ideas and resources from the guide and including them in their own schemes of work.

● Preparation

How many films do I need to see?

In general – the more, the better. We have already suggested that you need to watch the focus films listed above, but naturally we recommend seeing as many films from as many cultures as you can. You should develop the habit of watching films with critical analysis in mind at all times. This will help you to develop your critical eye and your fluency in film language.

Equipment

The language of film can be taught with fairly minimal resources. A TV set, a VHS video player and some films on videotape are enough. However, a number of other resources can enhance the experience considerably for your students.

● A DVD player

These offer many valuable features: extremely high quality; correct (or near-correct) aspect ratio; precise freeze-frame and slow motion; and extras such as director's commentary tracks. A DVD player is now a near-essential resource for film and media teaching. For advice on setting up DVD output, see the notes on setting up your DVD correctly for widescreen TV at www.bfi.org.uk/tfms.

● **A widescreen TV**

Especially when working with large groups, the larger the screen, the better.

● **An electronic whiteboard and data projector**

This will allow you to project your films on an impressive scale, and by using a computer with a DVD drive and the appropriate software, you will also be able to freeze-frame and use the pens to draw onto the frozen image – very useful for highlighting elements of framing and staging. This is an excellent resource, but we would offer two words of warning. Firstly, the built-in sound tends to be very poor, so you should also make the fairly modest additional investment in an amplifier and speakers; secondly, you will usually require blackout blinds, which can be very expensive.

● **A laptop or other computer with DVD drive**

An excellent tool for one-to-one tutorial work, or for preparing close analysis of a sequence. You, or your students, can also use DVD software to capture stills, which can really illuminate a written analysis or presentation. If you are setting up a desktop PC for film analysis, we recommend two monitors, a DVD-RW drive, the fastest processor and the largest amount of memory you can afford.

● **A good library of books on film language**

The bibliography in this guide should provide a solid start. A copy of Bordwell and Thompson's *Film Art: An Introduction* (2004) is essential. For use in the classroom, and by teachers who are unfamiliar with the basics of cinematography, we highly recommend Jeremy Vineyard's *Setting Up Your Shots* (2000) as a simple, well-illustrated guide to the main camera techniques and their effects on the audience.

● **Some general approaches to teaching film language**

Particularly when you are working with students who are thinking about the technical language of film for the first time, the volume of knowledge to be communicated can seem overwhelming. However, for your students, this is not a foreign language. Most people in the West are steeped in the conventions of Hollywood storytelling from an early age. They already understand them, and so your task is to illuminate and codify their instinctive knowledge. Teaching the technical language of film is unique in that you will almost exclusively be giving your students the vocabulary to explain things they already know, rather than providing them with new concepts. This can be an exciting and empowering experience. Students often gleefully report to us that they now 'can't watch a film without taking it apart'.

Some students, particularly if they are convergent thinkers, can be hostile to the idea of this type of analysis. In the early stages, such students need to be convinced of the value of repeatedly viewing a sequence. Usually, after working through a few analyses, most students do come to understand the depth and complexity of even very simple film sequences, and that they require very careful attention to detail. The activity based on *Smoke* is an excellent starting point. See www.bfi.org.uk/tfms: **Student notes: Shot structure in *Smoke*.**

Ultimately, we are aiming to make our students into independent, critical readers of film language, able to analyse without the direction of the teacher. The best general approach begins with teacher-led analysis of a scene with the class and ends with an individual analysis by the students. Pair work and group work are good ways to bridge these two stages. It is also essential that you prevent the learning process from becoming overly passive and teacher-centred. Rather than showing and explaining a stream of film extracts, look for ways to engage your learners actively and creatively. **Worksheets 7, 8** and **9** give ideas for varying the classroom experience.

You can also modify the experience of analysing a sequence in numerous ways. For example:

- Mute the sound during a showing (a) to emphasise visuals, and (b) to reveal the contribution of sound to the final sequence;
- Provide the script for the sequence (many are downloadable from www.script-o-rama.com) and have students try to predict the way it will be filmed – through discussion or a storyboarding exercise;
- Compare a radio version of a sequence (many are commercially available on CD, *Star Wars* for example) with the original film. What compromises have been made?

The most important aspect of preparation is that you should feel confident about the sequence you are exploring with the class, but not become dogmatic. With a little practice, most people can develop the ability to identify the intended meanings and messages within a film, and the ways in which the filmmakers seek to create them. However, you should never forget that the meaning of a film lies in the experience of the spectator, at least as much as it does in the intentions of the director. This means that with a new sequence, we should always begin by asking students what it means, rather than by telling them.

As far as possible, you should be exploring the sequence with the class, rather than guiding them through territory that you have mapped exhaustively. For this reason, we prefer to introduce new sequences and new films to our teaching as often as possible, rather than repeating the same ones every year. Especially in the early stages of teaching film language, it is useful to consider some pieces that you know extremely well, but this is not an approach we would recommend once learners have begun to develop their skills. If you are new to this type of work you might balk at the idea of having students bring in their own choices of extract for unprepared analysis in the classroom. However, this level of fluency in film language ought to be your ultimate aim: not least because it is what you will expect from your students. This guide is intended, and structured, to help build such fluency.

● Theoretical perspectives

In general, at this level, we would encourage students to discover their own structures of meaning within a film, rather than relying too heavily on theorists. Too often at A Level, sophisticated theories are boiled down to their very basic elements, and consequently they cease to have much meaning.

In this guide, we have tended to step away from theoretical perspectives. Where it seems to us that theories are useful, as is certainly the case with Roland Barthes' codes of enigma and action, we raise them.

● Assessment strategies

To a great extent, the assessment strategies you choose will probably be determined by the type of course you are teaching. Students working towards a coursework essay will need to be assessed in very different ways from those who are preparing for an examination. However, the general pattern of moving towards greater independence holds true in all cases. Taking what is perhaps one of the more difficult tests, we can look at this process in operation.

Recent years have seen a trend towards testing students by presenting them with a previously unseen moving image extract, which they must analyse under exam conditions. Scheme of work 2 describes a typical process by which a group could be led from having no previous knowledge of film language through to this rather challenging assessment. If you are delivering the OCR or CCEA specifications, or feel that an unseen extract exam might be a useful addition to your scheme of work, we have included advice on setting up unseen moving image examinations at www.bfi.org.uk/tfms.

Scheme of work 1: Micro analysis of *Donnie Darko*

Possible exam board focus: WJEC Film Studies AS Level (Unit FS1)

Time: Five weeks (four hours per week)

Aims:
On completing this unit, students should be able to:
● Understand the use of cinematography, *mise en scène*, editing, sound and SFX in *Donnie Darko*
● Explain how these elements create meaning in specific scenes

- Apply these concepts to scenes in other films

Outcomes:
- A coursework essay analysing a five-minute sequence from *Donnie Darko* or another film
- Skills of close textual analysis that can be used in any aspect of Film Studies

Week 1 Introduction
Brainstorm 'adolescence'. Discuss: In what ways is adolescence different from other stages in life?
Viewing of *Donnie Darko*
Elicit initial responses. Interpretation exercise – **Worksheet 19**
Consolidate interpretations on board

Week 2 Cinematography and *mise en scène*
Camerawork – students film various shots using glossary
Composition – **Worksheet 20**
Mise en scène – analysis of look of *Donnie Darko*
Research exercise – **Worksheet 21**

Week 3 Editing and sound
Discussion – the relationship between the original cut, the DVD edition and the director's cut
Close analysis of the scene in which time is reversed and the scene in which Donnie gets suspended
Sound – discuss the uses of the soundtrack – **Worksheet 22**

Week 4 SFX
Elicit response to the liquid spears in the film – what do they mean?
Discussion – the value of SFX in film
The dream sequence – **Worksheet 23**
Close analysis sequences – 'Average School Day' (teacher-led) and 'Cellar Door' (pair or group work)

Week 5 Coursework
Analyse opening scenes from other films
Students work on individual analysis and essay, either for *Donnie Darko* or another film

Scheme of work 2: Unseen textual analysis

Possible exam board focus: OCR Media Studies AS Level Media Studies (Unit 2731)

Time: Six weeks (four hours per week)

Aims:
On completing this unit, students should be able to:
- Learn the skills needed for close textual analysis
- Explore how film language creates meaning
- Apply this knowledge under timed exam conditions, using appropriate terminology

Outcomes:

- Personal glossaries of film language concepts
- Skills of close analysis that can be used in any aspect of film or media studies
- Accounts of three sequences produced by students

Week 1 Introduction to film production and film language
The three stages: pre-production, production, post-production
Worksheet 2: Film credits: What do they mean? What happens and when in the filmmaking process?
The three main elements of film language – *mise en scène*, cinematography, editing
Smoke closing sequence: a comparison of film storytelling in two forms (**Student notes: Micro language and narrative – an analysis of *Smoke***)

Week 2 Exploring film language
Students use video camera to experiment with various types of shot (**Worksheet 9**)
Present results to class and discuss effects
Die Hard 3 Storyboarding activity (**Worksheets 10a and b**)

Week 3 *Die Hard 3*
Students view whole film, watching out for the sequence they have storyboarded
Discuss: What makes this sort of film successful with audiences?
Using robbery sequence and **Worksheets 12.1–12.8**, discuss operation of film language throughout this sequence
Students fill in gaps in DIY glossaries as the week progresses
Set task for next week: choose a sequence for detailed micro presentation

Week 4

Prepare and present detailed micro analyses to the class (**Worksheet 11**)

Week 5 *Spider-Man 2* – extract only

Using **Worksheet 24** in small groups, produce detailed analytical notes on the 'Theatre' sequence

Based on this analysis, write an account of the sequence in 60 minutes under test conditions

Week 6

Apply **Worksheet 25** to an unseen sequence, eg the chase from the arcade to the conduit in *Terminator 2: Judgement Day*

2

Background

The following are the basic concepts used to approach any study of film language:

- Genre
- Narrative
- Production processes

The first two concepts are detailed from page 22. Before we proceed, however, it is useful to outline some of the main ways in which production processes and decisions construct meaning.

Production processes

● Pre-production

The first stage in the creation of a film is the assembly of an idea and a script. Sometimes this is a fully developed screenplay; sometimes it is little more than a basic pitch, in which the writer describes the script s/he will write if the producer agrees to supply the funding. This script will influence many of the macro aspects of film language, such as character development, themes and narrative tension. However, it is common for scripts to be rewritten, sometimes beyond recognition, during pre-production.

Casting is a critical element of pre-production. The director is one of the first people appointed, and s/he has the most significant influence over all elements of the film from then onwards. The director and casting director do most of the casting of main actors. Supporting players are usually found by the casting director alone. Star power is very strong in Hollywood, and this means that the leading actor is sometimes involved in production, and may even select the director. However it is achieved, casting is very important in creating meanings within the film. This is not just because an actor has a particular look or style, but also because s/he may bring a certain star identity to the role. For example, casting Renée Zellweger as a romantic lead will create very different meanings from casting Julia Roberts in the same role.

At this stage, some elements of the film's overall look are also constructed. The art director or the production designer works with costume and set designers to create a consistent aesthetic tone for the film. Location scouts search for appropriate places to film. Storyboards are prepared for important sequences.

Special effects work begins during pre-production, since computer-generated images and animatronics can be extremely time consuming. Miniatures, puppets and prosthetics are built.

● Production

During the period when a film is shot, the elements of film language prepared in the pre-production stage are assembled into real footage. Under the guidance of the director, the actors perform their roles for the camera. The director of photography (DP), or cinematographer, is one of the most important people at this stage. In consultation with the director, s/he sets up camera moves, instructs the lighting crew and composes the shots we eventually see.

Some special effects are constructed at this stage. Pyrotechnics and stunts are filmed on set. Chroma key sequences are shot in special studios.

● Post-production

At this point, editing and sound become the main focus. The editor cuts the filmed footage into a meaningful sequence. The language of film is composed of many elements, but most important of all these is the edit. As a crude analogy, think of cinematography as making the visual equivalent of words; film editing arranges those words into sentences, paragraphs and chapters.

During production, the only element of sound anyone is interested in recording is the dialogue. This means that, apart from the lines spoken by the actors, virtually the entire soundscape of a film is normally constructed in post-production. (Students often find this difficult to comprehend, but there are now many DVD bonus documentaries exploring the creation of sound for films. A very accessible one is included on the second disc of *Spider-Man 2*.) The key players are the sound design department, the foley artists and the composer. Students must recognise that every sound in a film is a decision, a message to the audience.

This is also the time when the final elements of special effects are created. Animated sequences are mixed with live action.

Macro analysis: genre and narrative

● Focus film: *High Noon*

To illustrate the key concepts of genre and narrative, we have used *High Noon* as a focus film. Made after the Paramount decree of 1948, which saw the break up of the Hollywood studio system, the film is useful as an example of both the studio-born Western and the freedom granted by new independent production companies, such as that owned by Stanley Kramer, the producer of *High Noon*. As a consequence, the otherwise classic narrative of *High Noon* is not only innovative in its use of real time and creation of suspense, but also in its subversion of the conventions of the Western genre.

● Genre

A genre is a type of film (eg horror, war, romantic comedy and, arguably, *film noir*), but it is also a system of signs used by producers, filmmakers and audiences to make meaning. A specific genre can be defined by typical plots, characters, themes and cinematic techniques. The plot of a romantic comedy, for example, usually involves a man and a woman overcoming a series of obstacles before they get together at the end. More often than not, a horror film is characterised by low lighting, dramatic music and a monster.

Genres exist in the film industry for a number of reasons:

- In the past, producers have capitalised on successful formulas by repeating them in a slightly different format.
- Producers are able to differentiate their product and target specific audiences – eg gangster movies for men, romantic comedies for women, teenpics for teens.
- Within a studio context, the production of genre films is more economically efficient. Sets, costumes and props can be used again; camera crews grow more adept at filming set sequences; and star images are developed to fit plot formulas. This was particularly true under the Hollywood studio system.
- Audiences are more likely to pay money to see a film if they know what to expect. Consequently, marketing will often emphasise generic elements.
- Genre provides a framework which a director (or equivalent) can use to express his/her individual style and themes.
- It is also a way for audiences and reviewers to differentiate between films.

As we can see, genre has been used by the industry to create marketable films since the days of the Hollywood studio system. As a genre is a commercial product, however, there has been a lot of debate as to how useful or appropriate it is to apply the concept to an academic study of film or film language. This debate is part of a wider concern running right through media and cultural studies that genre analysis tends to limit the ways in which the meanings of texts can be explored. TV, radio and publishing, as well as art and literature, can all be approached via genre, but many critics are uncomfortable with this method.

On the other hand, as Jacques Derrida has written, 'there is no genreless text' (Derrida, 1981, p61). In other words, every text, and every film, fits into a genre. Audiences experience texts as parts of genres, so genre must be recognised to be an important element of film language. Rick Altman's sophisticated account of the subject in his 1999 book *Film/Genre*, which explores both the strengths and weaknesses of this approach, is required reading for anyone who wishes to develop a better understanding of film.

From the point of view of teaching students how to read films, it is essential that they are able to recognise the ways in which producers, filmmakers and audiences use genre features as shorthand to create meanings within a film. Once they are confident with the idea of genre, it can be both useful and interesting to question generic approaches, but it is usually best in the early days to treat it as a straightforward concept.

For example, to understand genre as an element of film language, it is important that students grasp the idea that films both repeat and differ from genre conventions. This process is known as repetition and difference.

● Repetition and difference

As we have noted, producers re-use successful formulas, but with variations so the audience don't get bored. On the one hand, audiences enjoy the familiarity of genre films. On the other, much of the pleasure of watching a genre film is in its variation from what is considered by the audience as the norm. Indeed, an auteur (a director with his/her own individual style and themes) might use the genre as a vehicle for self-expression, or else subvert the genre and its meanings through a more radical departure from convention.

As a result, the conventions of genre are not fixed, but evolve over time, usually in line with changing audience expectations and attitudes. For example, *Butch Cassidy and the Sundance Kid* (George Roy Hill, USA, 1969) recreated the Western for the 1960s, abandoning the clear moral agenda of earlier films in the genre and offering instead freewheeling, hedonistic central characters and hippy ideals. Similarly, in *House of Games* (David Mamet, USA, 1987), the characteristic gender roles of *film noir* are reversed so that a female investigator is seduced by an 'homme fatal', reflecting the changing roles of women and men in the 1980s. It is through this evolution, then, that meaning is produced.

Focus film: A comparison between *High Noon* and a more conventional Western released in the same year, *The Duel at Silver Creek* (Don Siegel, USA, 1952) starring Audie Murphy, illuminates the effect these differences can have on audiences. Audiences of *High Noon*, for example, would have noted the following:

- The stark, black and white, documentary quality to the cinematography compared to the pretty look of most Westerns at the time;
- The small scale compared with the epic and/or panoramic sweep that the audience would expect;
- The emphasis on suspense and the deferment of action until the end;
- A hero who admitted he was afraid.

As we can see, the response of the audience depends on their knowledge of other Westerns. As they watch the film, they tend to compare it with other film texts. This process of making meaning through connections with other texts is referred to as intertextuality. It is an aspect of our experience of all genres, but it is sometimes used by filmmakers in a more self-conscious way. For example, in *Brief Encounter* (David Lean, UK, 1945), Laura (Celia Johnson) and Alec (Trevor Howard) see a cinema trailer for an imaginary film, *Flames of Passion*. By referring to this very conventional romance within the film, characterised by extreme passion and exotic locations, Lean emphasises the realism of *Brief Encounter* compared to other films in the genre.

To explore these ideas with a class, see **Worksheet 4**.

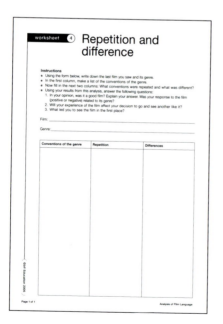

To access worksheets and other online materials go to **www.bfi.org.uk/tfms** and enter User name: **filmlang@bfi.org.uk** and Password: **te1306fl**.

● Iconography

It is through repetition that a genre develops its iconography. Bordwell and Thompson define iconography as 'recurring symbolic images that carry meaning from film to film' (*Film Art*, 2004, p111). The term normally refers to objects and settings – in Westerns, the six-shooter, the horse, the desert landscape – but can also be the physical attributes of an actor or star – the rugged face of John Wayne, for instance. Indeed, with its roots in silent film, when filmmakers told the story primarily through images, the visual iconography of the Western is particularly pronounced. All genres, however, depend on the audience making certain associations with images. For example, in gangster movies such as *The Public Enemy* (William A Wellman, USA, 1931), the Tommy gun is associated not only with violence but also with the breakdown of law and order in American society during the 1930s.

Through iconography then, information is passed quickly and economically to the audience in order to communicate aspects of character or setting. A tin star badge in a Western will instantly establish the authority of the sheriff; and the rolling tumbleweed in spaghetti Westerns conveys the harsh and inhospitable landscape the characters inhabit. Iconography can also be used as a narrative device to create suspense. Saloon doors swinging open tell the audience that there is going to be a violent confrontation. If an icon is overused, however, it will become a cliché and lose its power, as this last example demonstrates.

A director can also use iconography to generate alternative or subversive meanings.

Focus film: In *High Noon*, for example, the crude colour symbolism of the traditional Western, where white equals 'good' and black equals 'bad', is reversed so that Marshal Will Kane, the hero, played by Gary Cooper, is dressed in black and Frank Miller, the villain, is dressed in lighter colours. Through his subversion of this conventional iconography, Zinnemann is foregrounding the moral ambiguity of the central character. Is Kane staying in the town out of moral duty or male pride? This is accentuated through the hero's oscillation between two iconic characters – the 'good' Amy Fowler, dressed in white and played by the young, fresh-faced Grace Kelly, and the 'bad' Helen Ramirez, dressed in black and played by the Mexican actress, Katy Jurado, as well as two iconic settings – the church and the saloon. This positioning is complicated further when, as we shall see, the meanings associated with these poles of good and bad are also disrupted.

To explore iconography and its use in *High Noon* with a class, see **Worksheets 5a**, **b** and **c**.

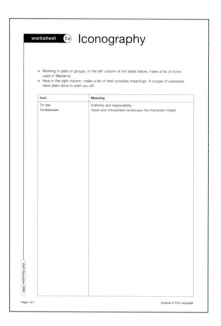

worksheet **5a** Iconography

- Working in pairs or groups, in the left column of the table below, make a list of icons used in Westerns.
- Now in the right column, make a list of their possible meanings. A couple of examples have been done to start you off.

Icon	Meaning
Tin star	Authority and responsibility
Tumbleweed	Harsh and inhospitable landscape the characters inhabit

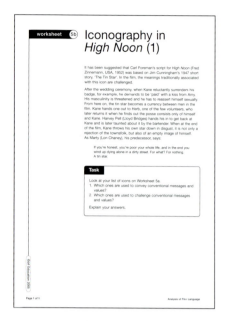

worksheet **5b** Iconography in *High Noon* (1)

It has been suggested that Carl Foreman's script for *High Noon* (Fred Zinnemann, USA, 1952) was based on Jim Cunningham's 1947 short story, 'The Tin Star'. In the film, the meanings traditionally associated with this icon are challenged.

After the wedding ceremony, when Kane reluctantly surrenders his badge, for example, he demands to be 'paid' with a kiss from Amy. His masculinity is threatened and he has to reassert himself sexually. From here on, the tin star becomes a currency between men in the film. Kane hands one out to Herb, one of the few volunteers, who later returns it when he finds out the posse consists only of himself and Kane. Harvey Pell (Lloyd Bridges) hands his in to get back at Kane and is later taunted about it by the bartender. When at the end of the film, Kane throws his own star down in disgust, it is not only a rejection of the townsfolk, but also of an empty image of himself. As Marty (Lon Chaney), his predecessor, says:

If you're honest, you're poor your whole life, and in the end you wind up dying alone in a dirty street. For what? For nothing. A tin star.

Task

Look at your list of icons on Worksheet 5a.
1. Which ones are used to convey conventional messages and values?
2. Which ones are used to challenge conventional messages and values?

Explain your answers.

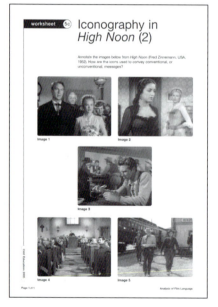

worksheet **5c** Iconography in *High Noon* (2)

Annotate the images below from *High Noon* (Fred Zinnemann, USA, 1952). How are the icons used to convey conventional, or unconventional, messages?

Image 1   Image 2

Image 3

Image 4   Image 5

To access worksheets and other online materials go to **www.bfi.org.uk/tfms** and enter User name: **filmlang@bfi.org.uk** and Password: **te1306fl**.

● Plot

A genre can also be defined by conventional storylines. Often a gangster movie will chart the rise and fall of a criminal, as exemplified by *Angels with Dirty Faces* (Michael Curtiz, USA, 1938) or *Goodfellas* (Martin Scorsese, USA, 1990). Similarly, an action adventure film will nearly always involve the hero completing a dangerous mission – the James Bond films are an obvious example. According to the screenwriter Frank Gruber, there are only seven basic Western plots:

1) The Union Pacific Story, centring around the construction of a railroad, telegraph or stagecoach line or around the adventures of a wagon train;
2) The Ranch Story with its focus on conflicts between the ranchers and rustlers or cattlemen and sheepmen;
3) The Empire Story, which is an epic version of the Ranch Story;
4) The Revenge Story;
5) Custer's Last Stand, or the Calvary and Indian Story;
6) The Outlaw Story;
7) The Marshal Story.

(See Gawelti, *The Six-Gun Mystique*, 1984, pp61–2)

Focus film: *High Noon* is an instance of 'the Marshal Story', but it also incorporates elements of 'the Revenge Story' and possibly even 'the Empire Story'. Alternatively, the film critic, Will Wright describes *High Noon* as a 'transitional' plot in which 'the hero is forced to fight against society' and the heroine 'joins him in his fight' (*Sixguns and Society*, 1975, pp74–5). In this way, the evolution of the Western plot in *High Noon* can be explained as reflecting the changing society of the 1950s.

This relationship between a plot and its historical context is true of any genre. Mid-20th-century spy thriller plots were driven largely by Cold War politics and, today, the terrorist plot is increasingly common. *The Sum of All Fears* (Philip Alden Robinson, USA, 2002), in which there is a nuclear attack by terrorists that destroys much of Baltimore, was extremely popular with American audiences.

To explore how plot is used in the Western genre, see **Worksheet 6**.

To access worksheets and other online materials go to **www.bfi.org.uk/tfms** and enter User name: **filmlang@bfi.org.uk** and Password: **te1306fl**.

● Character types

A genre film also uses stock characters or types that fit into these plot formulas. The action-adventure film, for example, will probably include a hero, a sidekick, a heroine and a villain. The male and female romantic leads in romcoms usually have less attractive best friends. Even in an arthouse film such as *Donnie Darko*, the director acknowledges that he is using 'archetypes' – Kitty Farmer in her beehive hairdo, the bald Principal Cole in his suit (DVD commentary). Within a genre – in this case, the high school movie – types have become an accepted part of film language.

Focus film: In *High Noon*, the Western types used are as follows:

● Marshal Will Kane – the lawman and hero, highly individual and morally ambiguous;
● Frank Miller and his gang – the outlaw and his posse, the archetypal villains;
● Amy Fowler Kane – the East Coast school teacher type, a moral and civilising force;
● Helen Ramirez – the '"Dark Lady" of the South' (Drummond, 1997, p76), a Mexican stereotype;
● Harvey Pell – the false hero, weak, cowardly and ambitious.

As the audience is familiar with these types, a filmmaker can establish their roles economically through casting, performance and costume. When casting *High Noon*, for example, Zinnemann was looking for 'an attractive, virginal-looking and inhibited young actress, the typical Western heroine' to play the part of Amy Fowler (cited in Drummond, p26). Grace Kelly, in her first major screen role, fitted the bill.

A type then is a character model, usually associated with a specific genre, used by a filmmaker to establish a role quickly within the short amount of screen time available. However, when this model conforms to an unjustifiably fixed mental picture associated with a particular social group, it becomes a stereotype. This is explored in more detail below.

● Representation

Stereotypes have the potential to reinforce conservative messages and values for a mass audience and portray minority groups negatively. The romance in romantic comedies is nearly always heterosexual, and the representation of black people in early Hollywood films is often either servile or comic. Traditionally, Westerns have reinforced stereotypes of gender and ethnicity. Men have been represented as hunters, explorers, fighters and protectors, and women as home-makers and peace-keepers. Similarly, Mexicans and Native Americans in Westerns have been portrayed as the savage 'other', a trend films such as *Little Big Man* (Arthur Penn, USA, 1970) and *Dances with Wolves*

(Kevin Costner, USA, 1990) attempted to reverse. Indeed, film also has the potential to challenge stereotypes and present a particular social group in a more positive or complex way.

Focus film: In *High Noon*, Zinnemann was only interested in establishing the female type of Amy Kane so he could challenge it. At the beginning of the film, we are invited to equate Amy's pacifism with her passivity and throughout her character is marked by inaction. In the final shootout, however, she enters the violent world of men. Killing James Pierce reverses the traditional roles of female captive and male rescuer. Furthermore, she aids Will in her own rescue. Interestingly, the feminist potential in Amy is given greater emphasis in the script. She is described by Carl Foreman, the scriptwriter, as being

> one of the new women of the period ... who are beginning to rebel against the limitations and restrictions of the Victorian epoch ... determined not to be a sheltered toy-wife but a full partner in marriage, and it is she who has planned their future. (Cited in Drummond, p54)

The character of Helen Ramirez also goes against type. Although a woman of her period, she is strong, independent, and subscribes entirely to the code of violence practised by the men. She questions Amy's pacifism and mocks Harvey for not being a man. She even hits Harvey when he forces himself on her; and, unlike Kane, she says she is not afraid of Miller. But as a Mexican character, typically portrayed as 'bad' in Westerns, she is shown to be 'decent' in her business dealings with Mr Weaver, despite the prejudices of his wife and the townsfolk.

Philip Drummond also points out that Kane is forced into a passive role for the majority of the film – waiting, watching and negotiating. The anxious, bruised and sweaty face of Gary Cooper signifies both his interiority and suffering – the opposite of 'the man of action' (Drummond, pp47–52). This passivity, however, is a meaning also created out of Cooper's star image.

● Stars

Star images are another generic convention associated with character that can be used by filmmakers. Arnold Schwarzenegger is associated with science-fiction action films such as *The Terminator* (James Cameron, USA, 1984); Ricky Tomlinson appears mainly in working class British tragicomedies like *Riff Raff* (Ken Loach, UK, 1990); and the Japanese actor Toshiro Mifune is associated with the *jidai-geki* or samurai film, as exemplified by *Seven Samurai* (Akira Kurasawa, Japan, 1954). Likewise, the meanings asscociated with John Wayne, Gary Cooper and Clint Eastwood are related to the Western genre. Filmmakers and audiences use these meanings created in previous genre films to establish characters in new films. In this sense, the creation of character through star image is another example of intertextuality as it relies on other film texts.

Focus film: When *High Noon* was released in 1952, Gary Cooper had already established a screen persona that was 'typically simple, thoughtful, moral, laconic, and direct' and 'associated with a powerfully solid and undemonstrative form of masculinity' (ibid, p21). The casting of Cooper is particularly interesting because, at the time, his star image was at a point of crisis. Drummond describes this phase in his career:

> He appeared briefly as himself in Marshall's musical extravaganza *Variety Girl* (1947) and in Butler's story about Hollywood, *It's a Great Feeling* (1949), while his contributions to Roy Del Ruth's *Starlift* (1951) and the omnibus picture *It's a Big Country* (1951) gently parodied the Western roles and ideologies with which he had come to be identified. These cameos reflect a period in which the values associated with the Cooper figure began to change and darken, and in which the character moved into middle age and isolation. (ibid, p23)

In comparison with other stars, Cooper was losing popularity – earning less and taking less at the box office. In addition, his personal life was at a low. He had separated from his wife and was suffering from health problems. The decline of Cooper's image as the Western hero, along with these events in his personal life, resonated with the character of Kane for 1950s audiences. Like Cooper, Kane is also at the end of his career and his marriage to Amy almost falls apart at the outset. Here, meaning is created, not only through reference to other films, but also other media texts such as newspapers, magazines and television.

To explore the relationship between the production context of *High Noon* and macro aspects of film language, see **Worksheet 7**.

To access worksheets and other online materials go to **www.bfi.org.uk/tfms** and enter User name: **filmlang@bfi.org.uk** and Password: **te1306fl**.

● Themes

As well as plot or character, a genre might also be defined by its themes. The gangster movie, for example, explores themes such as crime, loyalty and the American dream; and the science-fiction film is often concerned with the relationship between human beings and technology. Structuralist film critics, such as Will Wright, attempt to identify underlying thematic structures in a story as opposed to focusing on content or style.

Focus film: In his analysis of the 'transitional plot' of *High Noon*, for example, Wright identifies the following oppositions:

- Inside society/outside society (the individual versus society)
- Good/bad (morality)
- Strong/weak (masculinity)

These themes are typical of what Wright calls 'the classical plot', which *High Noon* differs from in a number of ways:

- Whereas the Western hero is usually an outsider who is welcomed by a town to help them in their time of need, Kane and Amy begin inside the society and are 'systematically separated from the town, first forcibly and finally by choice'. Thus the already uneasy relationship between the individual and society – a key theme of Westerns – is dramatically severed.
- Furthermore, unlike in a conventional Western where 'the hero and society were both "good"', in *High Noon* 'the town is the hero's real enemy, not Miller and his men'. In the light of this, the theme of morality – another key theme of Westerns – is re-examined.
- Finally, 'the society is depicted as firmly established and collectively strong, capable as a group of defeating the hero', whereas normally the hero is strong and the townsfolk are weak. The reversal raises questions relating to the theme of masculinity in Westerns (*Sixguns and Society*, pp75–6).

Although *High Noon* explores themes typical of the Western, the way it explores them is significantly different from previous models.

● Cinematic techniques

Sometimes genre can also be defined by the techniques that are used. This is particularly true of *film noir*, characterised as it is by interior settings, low-key lighting and unconventional camera angles, but it is also true of the Western.

Focus film: The way *High Noon* differs in its construction from conventional Westerns is as follows:

- In order to create a stark newsreel quality to the film, a distinctly realistic look compared to the picture postcard scenery of most westerns at that time, Floyd Crosby, the director of photography, decided not to use filters, soft focus or spotlights.

- The choice of interior, as opposed to exterior, settings created a feeling of claustrophobia and entrapment. With the exception of the title sequence and the scene when Kane and Amy leave town towards the beginning, the wide shot, a staple of most Westerns, is absent from the film.
- The use of the folk song written by Dimitri Tiomkin and Ned Washington was different from the orchestral fanfare usually heard at the beginning of Westerns.
- Harry Gerstad and Elmo Williams's innovatory climactic montage at high noon was unusually experimental for a Western film.

This use of cinematic techniques as a mark of difference is explored in more detail in the section on micro analysis. (See pXX)

● Hybrid genres

Finally, whereas genres evolved as a way of targeting particular audiences, hybrid or sub-genres evolved as a way of capturing a wider audience. Typically, a romantic subplot was introduced into a Western to appeal to a female audience as well as a male one. The mixing of genres may also be used as another variant. Examples include the science-fiction Western *Westworld* (Michael Crichton, USA, 1973) and the comedy Western *Blazing Saddles* (Mel Brooks, USA, 1974). Both these are useful as classroom resources in identifying the iconography and conventions of the genre.

Genre hybridisation has become an important element in trying to ensure that high concept Hollywood movies reach the largest audience possible. For example, *Spider-Man 2* includes elements of various genres, including horror, science fiction, action-adventure and indie romance.

● Narrative

A popular criticism of film is that it lacks depth. Filmmakers focus too much on telling the story and not enough on developing characters or exploring ideas. Student filmmakers will be aware how much time and effort it takes to film even the simplest scene. But we shouldn't necessarily assume that character and ideas are more valuable than the ability to tell a story with economy and precision. In film, narrative has become something of an art form and consequently is of particular interest to Film Studies students.

Propp and Todorov

The two most frequently cited theorists on narrative in Film Studies are Vladimir Propp and Tzvetan Todorov. In *Morphology of the Folk Tale*, Vladimir Propp identified 31 elements or 'morphemes', which he saw as being the basic ingredients from which all stories were created. These range from 'A family member leaves home or disappears' to 'The protagonist is married and ascends the throne'. They are listed in **Student notes: Propp: Morphology of the Folk Tale** at www.bfi.org.uk/tfms.

Tzvetan Todorov's idea of narrative structure has also been attractive to film academics. He suggests that there are three fundamental stages in every narrative. The story begins with equilibrium (the world in a state of balance and harmony), it then progresses through a period of disequilibrium (the world is temporarily disrupted and chaotic) before reaching the third stage of a new equilibrium.

Both of these structuralist approaches have their uses, but taken in isolation from the context of the production and the audience of the film, they are rather sterile. We could, for example, identify Propp's morphemes or Todorov's narrative stages in *The Full Monty* (Peter Cattaneo, UK, 1997) or *About a Boy* (Chris and Paul Weitz, UK/USA/France/Germany, 2002). Neither approach on its own would tell us much about the films' individual meanings or their effects on audiences. All it would tell us is that they share certain characteristics with other stories. On the other hand, if we considered the theme of masculinity in contemporary Britain, it would produce a much more meaningful account of each of these films.

● **The classic narrative**

Indeed, a more useful narrative model is one linked more explicitly to Hollywood film – the classic narrative. Although this is largely a convention developed during the Hollywood studio system (and *High Noon* is one example), Todorov's three narrative stages are a key feature. It should be emphasised, however, that it is still a term used by academics and not by people working in the industry. The key features of the classic narrative are as follows:

- The world portrayed is verisimilar – in other words, it is recognisable.
- The story begins in a state of equilibrium, a state of disequilibrium is created, until finally a new equilibrium is established (see Todorov above). These stages are sometimes referred to as the three 'acts' of a film: setup, complication and resolution.
- Events are organised into a cause-and-effect relationship.
- Events are caused by characters.
- There is a strong sense of narrative closure at the end.

(See Annette Kuhn in Cook and Bernink (eds), *The Cinema Book*, 1999, p40.)

Focus film: At the start of *High Noon*, for example, Kane and Amy get married, but their honeymoon and the peace of the town are disrupted by the news of Frank Miller's release, causing Kane to stay and look for help. At the end of the film, Kane kills Miller and is reconciled with Amy, but his relationship with both his wife and the town have changed.

While the classic narrative is primarily a convention of Hollywood cinema, it can be a useful starting point for any analysis of film, even if you conclude that the structure has been rejected. Although the narrative of *La Haine* (Matheiu Kassovitz, France, 1995) is clearly organised into a series of cause-and-effect relationships, it refuses to re-establish an equilibrium at the end and instead creates a new conflict in the final moment of the film. As a result, we do not leave the film feeling the issues of poverty, racism and gun violence have been resolved, but rather that French society, to use the words of the film, is in a state of 'free fall'.

● Plot and story

Another way of analysing how a narrative works is by dividing it into plot and story. Bordwell and Thompson define the plot as 'everything visibly and audibly present in the film before us' and the story as '[t]he set of *all* events in a narrative, both the ones explicitly presented and those the viewer infers' (*Film Art*, pp70–71).

Focus film: The main plot of *High Noon* can be summarised as follows:

● The Miller gang gather, enter the town, and wait for Frank Miller at the station.
● Kane and Amy get married, they learn about Miller's release, and Kane decides to stay.
● Kane looks for help. This constitutes a significant portion of the film.
● Meanwhile, Amy meets Helen, they talk, and ride to the station.
● Miller arrives and Helen leaves. There is a shoot out between Kane and Miller and his gang. Amy returns and kills Pierce. Kane kills Miller.
● As the community gather, Kane throws down his badge in disgust and leaves with Amy.

As well as the plot, however, the story includes events that are not shown on the screen but occur at the same time – for example, Frank Miller's journey to Hadleyville on the train. It also includes the pre-text or backstory – the events in the past that we learn about indirectly during the course of the film. For example:

● Miller committed murder and Kane captured him. Miller promised revenge.
● Amy Fowler's father and brother were killed in a violent confrontation. Consequently, Amy renounced violence and became a Quaker.
● Helen Ramirez had relationships with both Miller and Kane.
● Harvey applied for the job as the new Marshal but didn't get it. Kane may or may not have been the cause.

In keeping with Bordwell and Thompson's definition, there is a clear relationship between past (causes in the pretext) and present (effects). This information isn't communicated to the audience at the beginning, however. Once the narrative has been set in motion by the news of Frank Miller's release, Foreman fills in the gaps in our knowledge and provides us with additional information necessary for understanding the ending. In this way, a lengthy exposition of plot is avoided.

To explore the idea of story and plot, see **Worksheet 8**.

To access worksheets and other online materials go to **www.bfi.org.uk/tfms** and enter User name: **filmlang@bfi.org.uk** and Password: **te1306fl**.

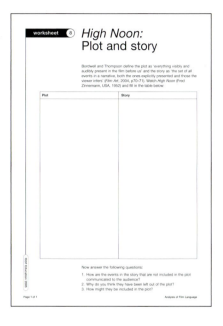

worksheet 8

High Noon: Plot and story

Bordwell and Thompson define the plot as 'everything visibly and audibly present in the film before us' and the story as 'the set of all events in a narrative, both the ones explicitly presented and those the viewer infers' (Film Art, 2004, p70–71). Watch *High Noon* (Fred Zinnemann, USA, 1952) and fill in the table below:

Plot	Story

Now answer the following questions:

1. How are the events in the story that are not included in the plot communicated to the audience?
2. Why do you think they have been left out of the plot?
3. How might they be included in the plot?

Page 1 of 1

Analysis of Film Language

● Diegesis

Another much-used term in the analysis of narrative is diegesis. This is a Greek word, meaning 'recounted story'. In most film narratives, the world of the story is presented to us as a self-contained reality. Characters live in a world and experience events, showing no knowledge that their doings are being witnessed by an audience. This world is known as diegetic reality. As viewers, there are some breaks with diegesis that we are accustomed to, and we accept these very comfortably without feeling that the realism of the film has been compromised. The most important of these are non-diegetic sound, especially soundtrack music or voiceover, and montage sequences. A technique that challenges our sense of diegetic reality more aggressively is the direct address of the audience, as used in *Alfie* (Lewis Gilbert, UK, 1965) and *High Fidelity* (Stephen Frears, USA, 2000).

Diegesis is also important to our understanding of time in films.

● Time

The temporal relationship between events can also be used to create meaning in a narrative. The two most common aspects to consider are order and duration (ibid, pp74–76). In a classic narrative, the order is usually linear or chronological, but a film might also use flashbacks – for example, *Citizen Kane* (Orson Welles, USA, 1941) – or a more experimental structure. A more recent example of the latter is Francois Ozon's *5 x 2* (France, 2004). Most probably influenced by the backwards narrative used in *Memento* (Christopher Nolan, USA, 2000), this rather bleak study of marriage begins with the couple signing their divorce papers and ends with them walking off into the sunset at the start of their relationship.

Temporal duration can also be important. Films often take place over long periods of time – this is particularly true of prison movies (see Case study 1, p63) – and so have to elide large portions of the story. As a result, the passing of time is conveyed to the audience through time codes. These might take the form of light levels (night, day), meals (breakfast, lunch, dinner) or costume (pyjamas, work clothes, evening dress). Alternatively, the passing of longer periods of time might be signalled by calendars or changes in the seasons; or longer still, the ageing of a character's body.

Focus film: The temporal structure of *High Noon* is conventionally linear, but, in terms of duration, the film occurs in real time. This makes the events more immediate and creates suspense, and the liberal use of time codes – the various shots of clocks – reinforces this experience for the audience.

● Narrative drive

Another important element of narrative is narrative drive. This can be defined as the techniques used by a filmmaker to capture and keep the attention of the audience. In most films, narrative is driven by conflict and ends when this conflict is resolved. This is particularly true of the classic narrative.

Focus film: The impending conflict in *High Noon*, for example, is foregrounded through the use of three key shots that punctuate the film at regular intervals:

- The static shot of the empty railway tracks, reminding the audience of the threat – the arrival of Miller on the 12 o'clock train;
- A travelling shot of Kane walking through the town, looking for help, his face marked with anxiety – another reminder of his fate;
- The shots of clocks, which are described by Zinnemann as 'looming larger as time slips by, pendulums moving more and more slowly until time finally stands still, gradually creating an unreal, dreamlike, almost hypnotic effect of suspended animation' (cited in Drummond, p35).

Through these shots the audience experience the tension felt by the hero.

As we have stated in the introduction, film language is a system of signs, and meaning is created through the interaction between the text and the audience.

This semiological approach to reading film is illuminated by an understanding of narrative codes. These are signs in a narrative that aid or promote reading and were first identified by the French semiologist, Roland Barthes. Although Barthes identified five narrative codes, we have found two particularly useful in the teaching of film language – action codes and enigma codes.

An action code tells us that something is going to happen. For example, in a science-fiction film, a flickering light often means an encounter with a supernatural or extraterrestrial being; and we have already noted how a saloon door opening predicts a violent confrontation. In both cases, the action codes work through the audience's familiarity with the genre.

Focus film: In *High Noon*, when the Miller gang ride through the town at the beginning, there is a sudden stab of music and a bit later, Ben Miller rears his horse outside the Marshal's office. On seeing the posse ride past, one character asks another, 'How many coffins we got?' In all three cases, the action codes signify trouble. The most powerful action code in *High Noon*, however, is the clock striking 12.

An enigma code, on the other hand, is a mystery in the text, a question that the audience want to have answered. This can work in relation to the overall narrative structure, as with detective narratives such as *The Maltese Falcon* (John Huston, USA, 1942), but it can also work within a given scene.

Focus film: In the title sequence of *High Noon*, for example, a number of questions are raised. Who are the men? Why are they gathering together? Where are they going? The answers to these questions lie further into the film, by which point more questions have been raised.

In summary, we have identified two ways in which narrative drive is created:

- Conflict and resolution
- Narrative codes.

Narrators and narration

Conventionally, the audience of a film is omniscient and sees and hears everything, but sometimes what we see and hear is limited to what is seen and heard by the central character, thus encouraging us to see the world of the film from his or her point of view. This is called a restricted narration. In addition to this, a character might tell the story using a voiceover, for example, the dead narrator of *Sunset Boulevard* (Billy Wilder, USA, 1950), or by talking directly to the camera, for example, Michael Caine in *Alfie*. In both cases, we are asked to recognise that what we see on screen is not an objective reality, but filtered through the consciousness of the narrator. In *Alfie*, for example, Michael Caine talks directly to the camera, but, as the film goes on, we realise that what seems like a frank and honest account of his sexual exploits is simply male bravado. Ironically, at the one point in the film when he is honest about his emotions and cries after the abortion, he turns away from the camera as if to hide from the audience. Audience positioning in relation to a character-narrator might be further manipulated through the use of point-of-view shots or other micro aspects of cinematography, *mise en scène*, editing, sound and SFX. As we shall see, a psychological interpretation of *Donnie Darko* is linked to film language in this way.

Micro analysis

As we suggest in the introduction to this guide, a micro analysis is a detailed textual analysis of the filmmaking techniques we can observe in a short extract from a film. It will be less concerned with the narrative or thematic development of the whole movie, or with any character's arc. It will look at the meanings created by film language within the sequence itself.

As Case study 2 on *Donnie Darko* shows, it can sometimes be impossible to achieve this degree of decontextualisation (see pp74–88). However, particularly with more straightforwardly generic movies, careful selection by the teacher can give students opportunities to analyse very self-contained extracts. You should look for sequences that can almost function as complete short films in themselves. We have chosen the main extract discussed in this section, and the sequence analysed in Case study 3 on *Spider-Man 2* (page 88), on that basis.

During the following account of Hollywood-style film language, we will refer in detail to a focus sequence: the robbery of the Federal Reserve in the action thriller *Die Hard: With a Vengeance*, which appears in chapter 5, beginning approximately 47 minutes into the current (cert 15) region 2 DVD version of the film. If you are using another version, you should be able to identify the sequence easily from the stills in the resource sheets. Throughout this guide, we will refer to this film by its alternative title of *Die Hard 3*. Additionally, we have provided a worksheet and webnotes based on a more unusual piece of filmmaking: the final sequence of the arthouse drama, *Smoke*. See www.bfi.org.uk/tfms.

Compared with analysis of genre and narrative, close (micro) analysis requires more reference to the technical elements of film production, it is still a semiotic process. In other words, what we must still emphasise are the meanings created by signs.

The language of film produces three types of response in the audience. It is useful to distinguish between these responses.

1. Film language may point the audience to a specific meaning.

Some techniques are the filmic equivalent of basic vocabulary. This sort of film language can be described as denotative. Its message is as clear as 'the cat sat on the mat'.

Focus film: See **Worksheet 12.4**. There is a point in the *Die Hard 3* sequence at which a bank guard notices that a group of businessmen are, incongruously, wearing military boots. This is presented to the audience through conventions of film language. A medium close-up of the guard allows his face to register slight puzzlement. We reverse to an eyeline shot of the boots, indicating that we are looking through his eyes. Then we reverse again for a reaction shot of the guard, who is clearly about to respond to what he has spotted.

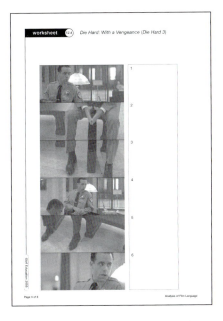

To access worksheets and other online materials go to **www.bfi.org.uk/tfms** and enter User name: **filmlang@bfi.org.uk** and Password: **te1306fl**.

Conventional editing and cinematography combine with elements of *mise en scène*, such as the guard's uniform and desk, the business suits and boots, to communicate a message that every spectator versed in Hollywood film language will understand in the same way.

2. Film language may produce an atmospheric or emotional effect.

These are more complex messages, and can be described as connotative. Usually, the filmmaker is trying to direct us towards a particular interpretation. The term for this process is 'anchoring preferred readings'.

Focus film: See **Worksheet 12.6**. Consider the murders of an anonymous guard and Felix Little (John C Vennema), later during the same sequence. Films in the action genre are usually replete with killings, and the audience cannot be allowed to feel the full emotional impact of every death, since this is essentially an entertainment genre. Here, the killing of the guard, which would have been hideous and distressing if shown realistically, is made less significant through shallow depth of field. The camera is focused on Felix, and the guard is killed out of focus. Casting, performance, costume and script all construct Felix as a ridiculous, pompous figure. By these means the vicious murder of his subordinate can be turned into a joke. Felix himself is then killed in a somewhat slapstick manner, as he is drugged and pushed over.

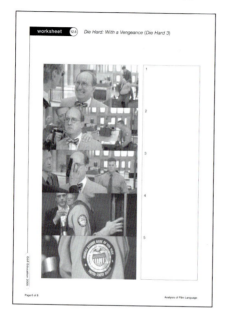

worksheet (12.4) *Die Hard: With a Vengeance (Die Hard 3)*

To access worksheets and other online materials go to **www.bfi.org.uk/tfms** and enter User name: **filmlang@bfi.org.uk** and Password: **te1306fl**.

3. Film language may trigger a range of more subjective and connotative reactions.

Again, the filmmakers will attempt to anchor preferred readings. However, there is more likely to be room for individual response by the spectator.

Focus film: The non-diegetic use of the tune 'When Johnny Comes Marching Home' to accompany the activities of the robbers will mean different things to different sections of the audience. For some spectators, it merely reinforces the military style of the robbery. Others will see it as ironic that this distinctively American melody is used as a theme for the apparently anti-American bank robbers. It may suggest that they are not exactly as they appear at first sight.

● Visuals

The three basic components of film language are *mise en scène*, cinematography and editing. A good way to begin understanding these terms is to consider them in chronological order as three stages in the production of a film:

1. The *mise en scène* is the thing that is photographed.
2. Cinematography is the process of filming the *mise en scène*.
3. Editing is the arrangement of the cinematographic material into a meaningful order.

Visuals 1: Mise en scène

Roughly translatable from the French as 'put in the scene', this term originally referred to the whole process of constructing a film. For the purposes of analysis at this level, we can take it to mean the arrangement and choice of elements to make up the picture. Perhaps the most obvious aspects of *mise en scène* are those elements of visual presentation which are organised before filming can take place: the pre-production work of art direction, set design, casting, costume and props.

In production and post-production, factors are introduced which can also be considered aspects of *mise en scène*. The cinematographic elements of lighting, depth-of-field, framing and composition all make up the picture we eventually see. Some editing and special effects techniques, such as superimposition, split-screen, dissolves and CGI also cross over into *mise en scène*. For students beginning to address film language for the first time, however, it is probably best to avoid such confusions, and keep the three categories very separate.

In its broadest sense, the language of *mise en scène* communicates essential information to the audience. Its commonest purpose is to create realism with regard to time and place. If the audience are to believe that they are looking at San Francisco in the year 2056, London in 1872, or Middle-Earth in the Third Age, the *mise en scène* should construct this. Genre is also frequently reinforced by *mise en scène*. This is most obvious in genres like the Western, historical drama or science fiction, where a world is created that is very different from that inhabited by the audience.

Having established the broad messages, an analysis of *mise en scène* can then be refined to consider more specific meanings. Casting decisions, the costuming of actors, surrounding details can all communicate a range of messages to the spectator, and are therefore open to semiotic interpretation.

Focus film: Worksheet 12.5. The *Die Hard 3* sequence in which Katya approaches and kills a bank guard demonstrates both broad and specific uses of *mise en scène* to create meanings. The sets, designed by Jackson De Govia, create a realistic representation of the interior of the US Federal Reserve Bank, based on thorough research during pre-production. There are heavy stone walls, iron cages filled with bullion, massive security doors and – essential both as a prop and for storytelling – CCTV screens. Costumes, for

41

example the uniforms of the guards, are used to help the spectator make important differentiations between characters.

To access worksheets and other online materials go to **www.bfi.org.uk/tfms** and enter User name: **filmlang@bfi.org.uk** and Password: **te1306fl**.

The casting of Sam Phillips as Katya is an entirely visual decision. Phillips is an American singer, but her look is strongly reminiscent of Marlene Dietrich. She is mute throughout the film because her accent would have contradicted the Germanic visual impression. She has been costumed in clothing that is both masculine and military. The effect, contradictorily, is to emphasise her female characteristics, and the audience are likely to see her as threateningly androgynous. Her character is being defined as conveying both female attractiveness and masculine violence.

She is given various props to enhance these effects. First we see her smashing into a wall with a pneumatic drill, a very phallic image. Next, the gloves and sunglasses that she drops as she walks suggest a striptease, reminding us of her femininity. Finally, we see the blade (specially designed for the film) in her hand; long, curved and sadistic, the prop symbolises and defines her character. Like her, it is an elegant killer. (See **Worksheet 12.8**.)

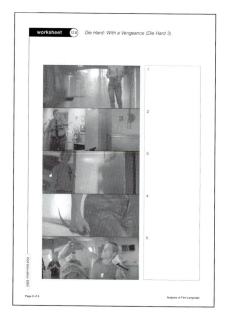

Further examples of *mise en scène* and its meanings are explored in the two case studies.

Visuals 2: Cinematography

The word cinematography literally means 'drawing movement', consequently some writers prefer the term 'cinemaphotography', which is certainly more accurate, but also rather unwieldy. This element of film production is arranged between the director and the cinematographer – often called the director of photography, DP or DoP. Some directors, notably Tim Burton and Ridley Scott, take more control than others over the photography, and many directors work repeatedly with the same cinematographers. Some of the most highly regarded films owe their look to a gifted DP such as Roger Deakins, whose style is usually rich, with a strong sense of pattern, as in *Kundun* (Martin Scorsese, USA, 1997) and *Fargo* (Joel Coen, USA, 1996). Similarly, *The Third Man* (Carol Reed, UK, 1949), voted the best British film ever by critics, depends for much of its disorientating effect on Australian cinematographer Robert Krasker's *film noir* lighting and canted camera angles.

An exhaustive discussion of professional cinematographic techniques is beyond the scope of this guide, and it is possible to be over technical. At this level, we are mostly interested in equipping students to explain what they see, and to consider its effects rather than to define the, often very complex, patterns of lighting and choices of lens that have produced the image. As teachers and as students, technical knowledge and vocabulary should enable us to articulate our responses more confidently and precisely, not to overwhelm and confuse.

Film stock

The starting point for determining the look of the finished film is the stock it is shot on. There is a range of film widths, from 8mm through to 70mm, with 35mm being the most common in professional use. Generally, the wider the filmstrip, the higher its quality and the larger it can be projected. However, the width is only one of many factors affecting the look of the projected image. Different brands of colour film produce different ranges of colour response, and lab processes can further modify this: washing out some colours, intensifying others. Some film appears more grainy and gritty; some appears smoother and softer. Moreover, a significant proportion of film now is not film at all but digital video, which is then processed electronically to create the look and feel of a particular film stock.

From the point of view of analysis, it might help to have a good understanding of the choice of stock and film processing. However, what we are most interested in is the final message. We merely need to ask the question, 'Does the quality of the film itself construct semiotic messages?' If it is grainy and harsh, what does that suggest about the sort of story we are being told? In *Bloody Sunday* (Paul Greengrass, UK, 2001), it helps to suggest that we are watching a representation of true events. Sometimes, film stock can serve particular narrative purposes. In both *21 Grams* (Alejandro González Iñárritu, USA, 2003) and *Memento*, switches in the appearance of the film stock (between lower and higher resolutions and between colour and monochrome) are used to help the audience distinguish between past, present and future events.

Lighting

John Alton's influential book on the *film noir* cinematography of the 1940s was called *Painting with Light*. This emphasised the importance of lighting to the construction of cinematic images. Lighting creates the mood and emphasises the key elements of *mise en scène*; it unifies the image and defines the composition. Lighting turns cardboard sets and plastic props into convincing three-dimensional reality and creates depth and meaning, but does not always draw attention to itself. Usually, like film music, lighting creates its effects without the audience noticing; sometimes, like film music, it becomes a dominating presence, as it does in *The Man Who Wasn't There* (Joel Coen, USA, 2001), for which DP Roger Deakins exaggeratedly, and beautifully, recreated the lighting of *film noir*.

Bordwell and Thompson offer a useful discussion of the three-point lighting system conventionally used in Hollywood. This approach is based on the idea that the figure should usually be lit from three directions:

● The key light – the main light source, creating the strongest sense of the direction of lighting;
● The fill light – softens the effect of the key light, and reduces shadows;
● The backlight – helps to make the subject distinct from the background.

As Bordwell and Thompson point out, the main purposes of Hollywood lighting are to focus our attention on important figures and to remove distracting shadows, and every new angle requires the repositioning of studio lights.

Focus film: The three-point system is the commonest approach to lighting straightforward dramatic scenes. Variations appear when required by realism and/or atmospherics – such as in the dark subway portions of the *Die Hard 3* sequence. You can contrast these with any of the interior close ups and two-shots from the upper portion of the bank, which are all lit using a typical high-key three-point system.

Once again, students should be less concerned with the techniques than with their effects, but it is essential that they are made aware that most film light is artificial. Thus, when a character switches off a light in a room, s/he is probably on a sound stage, and the effect is created by lowering the studio lights at the moment s/he flicks the switch. Sometimes, artificial light sources are used in an unrealistic, but necessary way. For example, compare any scene set inside a car at night to reality. Inside a real car in motion, there are no light sources; inside a movie car, everyone is illuminated, often from below, since otherwise the characters would not be visible to the audience. *Thelma and Louise* (Ridley Scott, USA, 1991) abounds with examples of this technique, which is especially noticeable in the Monument Valley sequence.

Even when natural sunlight might be sufficient for filming, either outdoors or through windows, it is usually too unpredictable to be relied on, especially when a scene can take several hours, several days, or longer to shoot. Only very infrequently do big budget filmmakers use unenhanced available light. Consequently, when we talk about 'ambient light' in a scene, what we really mean is that the filmmakers have created the impression of ambient light.

In **Worksheet 13** we have provided a variety of stills for class discussion.

1 of 2 pages

To access worksheets and other online materials go to **www.bfi.org.uk/tfms** and enter User name: **filmlang@bfi.org.uk** and Password: **te1306fl**.

The following questions about lighting will encourage a personal response from students:

a. What does the lighting reveal? What does it hide?

b. What does the lighting emphasise? What does it reduce in importance?

c. Does the lighting create contrasts between particular elements of the *mise en scène*?

d. Does the lighting create mood?

It is then possible to move on to more technical questions:

e. Does the lighting appear to be ambient or artificial?

In other words, are the filmmakers seeking to create the impression of natural sunlight or moonlight? Or is there an intended effect of electric, neon or gas lighting? For example, *Lost in Translation* (Sofia Coppola, USA/Japan, 2003) cleverly uses deliberately lifeless artificial light sources to convey the superficiality and tedium of hotel life.

f. Is the lighting high-key or low-key?

High-key lighting is the most common form used in Hollywood film. It produces an even spread of softer, rounded tones, making the detail within shadow areas more visible. High-key lighting is not confined to daytime shots. In night shots, the high-key system makes the scene visible throughout the full range of light and shadow. High concept films like *Die Hard 3* are usually lit in this way throughout. Low-key lighting produces the more dramatic, threatening shadow areas associated with *film noir* and horror movies. Typically, it creates strong contrasts between light and shadow areas, and much of the scene will be in darkness. The boat scenes in *The Usual Suspects* (Bryan Singer, USA, 1995) provide many excellent examples of this style.

g. Does the lighting produce soft, rounded forms or hard, flat ones?

The three-point lighting system creates a sense of depth and roundness which reinforces the audience's sense of realism. Sometimes, lighting is used to flatten forms, to create a more two-dimensional effect. Usually this would be for symbolic purposes. For example, the scene near the beginning of *American Beauty* (Sam Mendes, USA, 1999), in which Lester (Kevin Spacey) is interviewed by Brad (Barry Del Sherman), has been lit by DP Conrad Hall to produce a very flat surface. This emphasises the lack of depth and substance in Brad's character.

h. Is the light coloured?

Commonly, coloured filters (gels) are used to create the impression of a particular light source. For example, if characters are illuminated by candles, an orange light creates the illusion that these are the actual light source, rather than just props. Sometimes coloured light serves other purposes. The still from *Harry Potter and the Prisoner of Azkaban* (Alfonso Cuarón, USA/UK, 2004) shows a blue filter creating coldness (see **Worksheet 13**). Conversely, for a sauna scene in *The Thomas Crown Affair* (Norman Jewison, USA, 1968), the DP, Haskell Wexler, used red light to create an impression of heat.

Focus film: Coloured light is used repeatedly in the vault sections of *Die Hard 3* for realist purposes, to suggest electric lights, torchlight and so on. An interesting moment occurs when Katya's face is briefly illuminated by a red light (**Worksheet 12.5**). This is a realistic touch, but may also serve symbolic purposes, suggesting danger.

i. If artificial, does the light source appear to be inside or outside the frame?

A light source within the frame tends to close the composition, while a light from outside the frame opens it up (see the section on framing and composition below). Sometimes, a light source within the frame serves diegetic purposes. In a scene from *Jackie Brown* (Quentin Tarantino, USA, 1997) for example, Ordell Robbie uses a dimmer switch to turn off a standard lamp inside the frame, in order to murder Jackie in the dark.

j. Is there strong use of attached or detached shadow?

Attached shadows are those that are part of a figure or object. For example, the dark side of a person's face when s/he is lit from left or right. Detached shadows are separate from the figure or object. High-key lighting mostly seeks to obliterate detached shadows, which would be distracting for the spectator, and to soften attached shadows. Low-key lighting tends to emphasise detached shadows and to deepen attached shadow. Genres that favour low-key lighting often present detached shadows as a means of suggesting the sinister or melancholy. In a famous scene from *Nosferatu, eine Symphonie des Grauens* (F W Murnau, Germany, 1922) the approaching vampire is seen only as a detached shadow.

Cinematography: framing and composition

There is considerable vagueness in Film Studies about the difference between these concepts. At the introductory level, it is not worth worrying about the distinction. The traditional artistic concept of composition was created to describe completely static images such as paintings. Consequently, it is not really adequate when talking about film, which is usually in a state of change.

Framing suggests the placing of a frame around an image, cropping away elements that are offscreen and creating compositional relationships between the objects within the frame. Combined with *mise en scène* , it is the best way to describe cinematic composition.

The standard terms for framing are based on the filming of human figures. The basic types of shot are, in order:

- Extreme long shot (ELS)
- Very long shot (VLS)
- Long shot (LS) (also called wide shot/WS especially when a wide angle lens is used)
- Medium long shot (MLS)
- Medium shot (MS)
- Medium close up (MCU)
- Close up (CU)
- Very close up (VCU) (also called big close up/BCU)
- Extreme close up (ECU)

Worksheet 3 gives examples of Lee Van Cleef, framed at all these shot lengths during the final shootout sequence from *The Good, the Bad and the Ugly* (Sergio Leone, Italy/Spain, 1966).

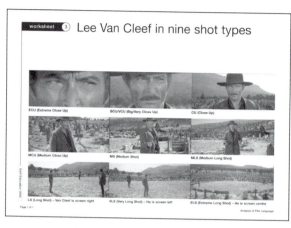

worksheet ③ Lee Van Cleef in nine shot types

ECU (Extreme Close Up) BCU/VCU (Big/Very Close Up) CU (Close Up)

MCU (Medium Close Up) MS (Medium Shot) MLS (Medium Long Shot)

LS (Long Shot) – Van Cleef is screen right VLS (Very Long Shot) – He is screen left ELS (Extreme Long Shot) – He is screen centre

To access worksheets and other online materials go to **www.bfi.org.uk/tfms** and enter User name: **filmlang@bfi.org.uk** and Password: **te1306fl**.

Since there are infinite distances a camera can be placed from a figure, these gradations are necessarily rather rough and ready in practice. For example, an MS would include something between 50% and 60% of a standing human figure – say, from the top of her head to the waist. A long shot would include 100% of the figure and some surrounding detail, but where the boundary lies between LS and VLS or ELS is relative to the context. When there are multiple figures within a scene, particularly when deep focus is used, are we looking at a CU of this figure or an LS of that one? Size of subject complicates things further: an MS of an adult would be an LS of a child at the same distance from the camera. When we start looking at non-human subjects, the whole system collapses completely. What, for example, would be a CU, MS or LS of a train?

The idea of shot length is useful to a certain degree, particularly when describing shots of adult human subjects, which are the commonest type of shot in narrative filmmaking. However, they almost always require some clarification in analysis. This can be achieved through detailed description, a frame sketch, or best of all a still. It is now very easy, using computer DVD drives, to capture frames from a sequence and either drop them into a word-processed essay or print them out. This reduces the necessity for description and allows students to concentrate on analysis.

Along with shot length, the main elements of framing are:

● Pattern – the arrangement of shapes and colours on the rectangle of the screen, considered as a two-dimensional surface. What is big? What is small? What colours dominate? In **Worksheet 3**, the final ELS is a highly symmetrical shot, dominated by the central oval of the foreshortened circle. The evenness of the pattern emphasises the ritual nature of the gunfight. It also suggests (falsely) that this is an equal contest.

- Weighting – an element of pattern. In American and European films there is a hierarchy in screen positioning, which is related to the way our written languages read left to right, top to bottom. Conventionally, the upper part of the frame is more powerful than the lower; screen right is weaker than screen left. Thus, as many feminist film critics have pointed out, in conventional presentations of men and women on screen, the woman would appear lower in screen right, the man higher in screen left.

  Focus film: In the *Die Hard 3* sequence, Felix Little is almost always placed in a weak screen position during his two shots with Simon (see **Worksheet 12.5**). When analysing films from cultures which use, for example, right-left script (such as Arabic), we should not assume the same hierarchy applies.

- Space – the placing of three-dimensional objects in relation to each other; what is in front of what? What is near? What is far away?

  Focus film: In the first shot of Katya (**Worksheet 12.5**), she is placed in the foreground to ensure that the audience identify her as the important figure. Surrounding players provide background detail.

- Angle – the position of the camera in relation to figures and objects. Do we look up at a character from a low angle, making her seem large and powerful? Do we look down on someone from above, making him small and weak? Is our view of a scene very flat, or do we approach it from left or right? Is the shot canted (tilted so that one side of the camera is higher than the other) to give us a sense of disorientation?

  Focus film: (See **Worksheet 12.7**.) In many of the shots of Simon (Jeremy Irons), we look up at him, to emphasise his leadership. In the second still, a low angle is used to reproduce the point of view of a captured bank guard.

- Movement – objects within the frame move, creating new arrangements within the frame and/or the frame itself moves (see the discussion of camera movement below), reframing the scene. For example, in **Worksheet 3**, the LS of Lee Van Cleef becomes the VLS because he walks deeper into the frame.

Additionally, framing can be open or closed. The open frame tends not to look too composed; it seems more informal, as if the camera has been pointed at a segment of life. A scene that is framed in an open way creates the impression that the world exists outside what we can see, beyond the frame. Closed framing looks much more formally composed. There is a sense of design and balance within the rectangle of the frame which creates an impression that the world we see is complete in itself. The films of Alfred Hitchcock provide many examples of closed framing, for example during the robbery sequence in *Marnie* (USA, 1964), and this strongly reinforces the themes of entrapment, fate and imprisonment that run through his work. Prison films, like those we discuss in Case study 1, often make use of closed framing for similar reasons.

Sometimes open framing is the consequence of a looser style of filmmaking, and the scenes are genuinely quite uncomposed; at other times it is a carefully constructed illusion. For example, if an interior is shot on a sound stage, open framing can remove the feeling of being studio bound. The audience have the impression that what they are looking at is a part of a wider world; there is a strong sense of off-screen space. In reality a pan too far to the left or the right, a tilt too far up or down, would reveal that we are not in a room at all but a three-walled set with no ceiling, surrounded by studio lights.

Aspect ratios

The most basic element of framing is the shape of the screen onto which the film is projected. The business of aspect ratios is much more clearly understood by audiences these days, since the development of widescreen television and DVD; and audiences in general are far more aware of the need to respect the director's original intentions. Nevertheless, there are still confusions and misapprehensions, which we will try to clarify here. Obviously, when analysing film language, the first stage is to show the film in its correct ratio, and to understand why it was chosen.

There is a very wide variety of original aspect ratios. The four we identify below are the commonest. See **Student notes** on **Common aspect ratios** for activities to encourage students to consider the effects of changing frame ratios at www.bfi.co.uk/tfms. (Enter user name: **filmlang@bfi.org.uk** and password: **te1306fl**.)

- Academy (4:3)

  This is the aspect ratio used in almost every film made before the 1950s. Until relatively recently it was also the shape of every television set and computer screen in the world. If you have an electronic whiteboard in your classroom, it will probably be this shape too.

  All film frames are around 4:3, no matter what aspect ratio the film is shot on. The different ratios are created either by use of mattes (which block off the top and bottom of the frame) or by anamorphic lenses (which squeeze a wider image into a narrower space).

- European widescreen (1.66:1)

  This ratio has been used for a large number of European movies, as well as several Disney films and much of Stanley Kubrick's output.

- American widescreen (16:9 or 1.85:1)

  This is now the commonest ratio for American films. It is also the shape of 'widescreen' TVs. The 1.85:1 ratio can fit a 16:9 TV screen (which is closer to 1.78:1) with minimal compromises.

- Scope anamorphic (2.35:1 and others)

  These very wide ratios have been made by a variety of processes, and include aspects ranging between 2.66:1 and 2.20:1. They tend to be used for large-scale, epic productions such as *The Fellowship of the Ring* (Peter Jackson, New Zealand/USA, 2001) or *Lawrence of Arabia* (David Lean, UK, 1962).

Aspect ratio as an element of film language

Usually, your interest in the aspect ratio should end with getting it correct for showing and analysing the film. There are, however, some instances in which the ratio becomes a distinctive element of the film's language.

The very wide scope ratios emphasise the horizontal plane, and tend to support compositions involving large numbers of characters and/or highly dramatic exterior locations. Thus, these ratios have become part of the accepted language of the epic, used to communicate the scale of the narrative, the isolation of the hero and so on. It is usually chosen to frame stories that are massive and heroic, rather than intimate and personal.

An exception to this general principle is *American Beauty*, a domestic story which was shot using Super 35 to produce a cinematic version in a ratio of 2.35:1. *American Beauty* exploits the tendency of wide ratios to seem very static. Mendes and his cinematographer Conrad Hall created symmetrical frames and avoided movement. Much of the film is composed of long takes, often combined with minimal camera and character movement. In this way, Mendes emphasised the movie's key themes of stillness and beauty.

Focus and depth-of-field

Cameras can be equipped with lenses of various focal lengths, and this gives the filmmaker control over what is or is not in focus at any time.

- Deep focus is used when the detail of an entire scene needs to be shown. It means that everything that is visible, near to and far from the camera, is in focus.
- Selective focus simplifies the image. It reduces the importance of certain elements within the frame by showing them blurred.
- Pulling focus, or racking focus, changes the subject of selective focus. See, for example, the killing of the guard and Felix in *Die Hard 3* (**Worksheet 12.6**).

Camera movement

The main purposes for moving a camera while filming are:

1. To reframe the scene;
2. To reveal new aspects of *mise en scène*;
3. To create kinetic energy;
4. To follow a character or object in motion;
5. To show the perspective of a character or object in motion.

We can categorise camera movements into five types:

1. Axis
2. Dolly
3. Vehicle
4. Aerial
5. Handheld

1. Axis movements

- Pans (rotation L-R or R-L on a vertical axis)

  These create the perspective of a static observer. For example, showing a cattle stampede, or a motor race, a panning camera movement would place the spectator in the position of someone being passed by. In establishing shots, a pan can be used to create the impression that we are taking a leisurely look around the landscape.

- Tilts (up and down or down and up on a horizontal left-right axis)

  These can serve various purposes. One is to reveal how tall something is. The camera is pointed at the ground floor of a building and then tilted up to show its full height. Another common tilt is the search up. We see a character's feet, then the camera tilts to reveal the rest of the character.

  Focus film: The *Die Hard 3* extract contains a less usual technique: a search down to show the military boots a character is wearing.

- Rolls (rotation on a horizontal front-back axis).

  These are the least common of the axis movements. Their classic use is to show the point of view of someone drunk, drugged, falling over in a daze or waking up.

2. Dolly shots

The camera is mounted on a 'dolly' or mobile support. Traditionally, dollies run on specially laid tracks for smoothness and precision, hence the term 'tracking shot'. A crab dolly, which does not require tracks, can be steered in any direction to give more flexibility. Mostly this has been superseded by steadicam. The third type is a crane dolly, used to create high-angle shots and massive, dramatic sweeping motions.

Focus film: In the *Die Hard 3* robbery sequence, a crane shot moves from overhead to ground level as Simon (Jeremy Irons) and his gang enter the bank. (See **Worksheet 12.2**.)

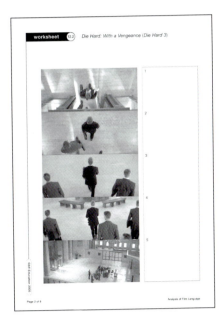

To access worksheets and other online materials go to **www.bfi.org.uk/tfms** and enter User name: **filmlang@bfi.org.uk** and Password: **te1306fl**.

Dollies are used for a massive variety of purposes. However, all of their movements are formed from combinations of:

- Track – moving along a horizontal plane;
- Crane up/down;
- Push-in/pull-out – moving nearer to or further away from a subject.

It is a common mistake in analysis to say that the camera 'zooms in' or 'zooms out' during a sequence. In fact, zoom – increasing the size of the subject using the lens – is relatively rare in professional filmmaking. Actual movement of the camera towards or away from the subject creates a different psychological effect. Pushing in feels as if we are moving nearer to the subject; zooming in feels more like it is being pulled towards us. Zoom draws attention to the fact that we are looking through a lens, while pushing in or pulling out seems far more natural.

Filmmakers are always looking for interesting ways to move the camera, and as soon as technology allowed, were experimenting with combinations of motion. Track and pan, pull back and tilt up, crane up and roll are fairly basic combinations. Using computer-controlled dollies, it is now possible to choreograph extremely sophisticated mixtures of camera movements. The large-scale action set-pieces that characterise high concept Hollywood cinema frequently utilise these new possibilities.

3. Vehicle-mounted shots

Placing the camera on board a moving car or van enables the filmmaker to show point of view from inside a moving vehicle, or to create a travelling shot from outside a moving vehicle. A genre that makes much use of these types of shot is the road movie. In *Thelma and Louise* many shots looking at the front of Louise's Thunderbird car in motion were created by towing the car from a van, on which a camera was mounted. Once the spectator is aware that this is how the shot was achieved, the illusion that Susan Sarandon is driving quickly vanishes. Films like *The Fast and the Furious* (Rob Cohen, USA/Germany, 2001) use vehicle-mounted shots to create excitement, putting the spectator into car chase sequences.

4. Aerial shots

The camera is mounted on a helicopter or aeroplane. This technique is sometimes used to film other airborne objects, such as planes; sometimes to shoot tall, dramatic objects, such as high cliffs and mountains, or cityscapes filled with skyscrapers. Michael Mann is particularly fond of this technique, and uses it repeatedly in *Collateral* (USA, 2004) to create a sense of the massive scale of modern Los Angeles.

5. Handheld shots

Handheld cameras give extra freedom of movement, and are sometimes used in action sequences. The disadvantage of the handheld camera is its unsteadiness. This is answered by the steadicam, which uses a gyroscope system to keep the shot more stable while the camera operator can be very mobile. The earliest use of steadicam in a Hollywood film was by Steven Spielberg for the boat sequences in *Jaws* (USA, 1975). Steadicam is also useful when the approach to filmmaking is more improvisational, and can create a lot of energy. Handheld work, whether using steadicam or not, is also good for creating a *cinema verité* or documentary feel. This is a technique used extensively in *The Bourne Supremacy* (Paul Greengrass, USA/Germany, 2004). The slight shakiness, even of steadicam work, has led to the industry slang term 'wobble shot' to describe this type of filming.

Focus film: The entry to the lower part of the bank as the lorries unload, in our *Die Hard 3* sequence, uses some very wobbly handheld work, to generate a sense of urgency and place the audience closely within the scene. This can be contrasted with the very smooth tracking work used on Simon and his men on the ground floor of the bank to create a feeling of tension.

Technological developments and camera movement

With the development of CGI (computer-generated images), it has become increasingly difficult to be certain just how much of what we see has been created with a camera, and how much is generated inside a computer, although sometimes DVD extras can be very revealing. There are times when it is more important than others to consider this issue. If we cannot easily tell, for example, whether a helicopter shot is 'real' or was created in a computer, then it makes most sense to consider it in terms of the effect on the audience. However it was constructed, we experience it as a helicopter shot.

On the other hand, a film like *The Matrix* (Andy and Larry Wachowski, USA, 1999) combines complex tracking shots with CGI effects to create sequences that would very obviously have been impossible to achieve in reality. Explicitly drawing the audience's attention to its own artificiality is a key element of the style and language of *The Matrix*, and so would be an important point for discussion of that film. Subsequently, many action movies have been influenced by the style of *The Matrix*. You can see such techniques in use in the James Bond film *Die Another Day* (Lee Tamahori, UK/USA, 2002) or the opening sequence of *Swordfish* (Dominic Sena, USA, 2001).

In *The Matrix*, artificial techniques were used to alter the language of film. This is different from the way George Lucas has operated in his *Star Wars* franchise. There, although much of the world he presents is created through special effects (using models in the first three films, CGI in the prequels), the style of camerawork is completely traditional.

Visuals 3: Editing

Mise en scène and cinematography are concerned with the organisation of space. Editing is the organisation of time. The editor's principal job is to make decisions concerning what we look at, in what order we look at it, and how long it is before we look at something else.

In most films, the primary purpose of editing is to create continuity – that is, a sense that the film makes logical sense in terms of immediate cause and effect, and is consistent in its presentation of the world. It is through continuity that the audience can believe in, and make sense of, the narrative. The following are the basic edits you are likely to encounter in Hollywood, or Hollywood-influenced film grammar.

- Master shot/master angle/safety shot
  This is the traditional way of ensuring continuity. The actors play the whole scene through from start to finish on one angle – a long or medium long shot. They then repeat their lines for close ups, two-shots and so on. The editor cuts all of this material together in the way that seems to work best.

- Montage editing
Material is filmed without a master shot. This requires the director to have pre-planned the edit to a much greater extent.

- Cut
One shot is replaced by another without any transition effects being used. This is the basic edit. There are several rules that ensure that cuts look smooth to the audience and do not 'jump' (see below).

- Cut-in

A close-up shot of an object or other small part of the preceding shot. This is used to draw attention to the significance of the object, or sometimes as a way of avoiding a jump cut.

- Cut-away

Used for similar reasons to the cut-in. A cut-away is a shot of any length, showing something that is in visible range of the preceding shot, but which did not appear in it, and is not part of a cause-and-effect sequence. For example an MS of a character sitting, looking at a campfire could be followed by a cut-away to the moon. However, if the character were shown looking at the sky, this would create an eyeline match, not a cut-away.

- Cross-cutting

Cuts repeatedly between two different locations or two characters/objects in motion. This suggests a relationship between them. For example that A is approaching B, or that what A is doing will affect B.

- Cross-fade/dissolve

One shot slowly replaces another, so that they are both temporarily present on screen at the same time. Usually used to suggest a relationship between the two images – eg the first character is thinking about the second.

- Reverse

A shot that is (or appears to be) presented at about 180 degrees from the preceding shot.

- Fade

Image gradually disappears and is replaced by a black (or other coloured screen). Sometimes used to suggest loss of consciousness. Traditionally used to communicate passage of time, though less common in modern cinema.

- Wipe

The new image is pushed across the screen, over the top of the previous one. This is a style of edit that draws attention to itself very strongly. Jill Bilcock's editing of the opening sequence for *Romeo and Juliet* (Baz Luhrmann, USA, 1996) includes a range of wipes.

- Graphic match

A cut emphasising something similar in the first and second images, usually by placing them in a similar screen position. Like dissolves, the graphic match is used to suggest a relationship between the two scenes.

- Match on action

A cut between two angles on the same action. For example, as Simon and his robbers enter the bank, we see him outside the door in **Worksheet 12.1**, and we then cut to the overhead shot of the interior, following the action in **Worksheet 12.2**.

● Eyeline match

We see that a character is looking in a particular direction. We then look from the character's POV. This is almost always followed by a reaction shot.

● Shot-reverse-shot

Used mainly as a convention of dialogue sequences. The point of view alternates between two opposite positions.

The main functions of editing are as follows:

Present events in the correct order

Usually this is normal chronology – time moves forwards from the beginning of the sequence to the end. However, there may be disturbances to the flow of time, such as flash forwards, as experienced by Richie (Adrian Brodie) in *Summer of Sam* (Spike Lee, USA, 1999), or flashbacks. Some editing technique is normally used to ensure that it is obvious to the spectator that we have temporarily left diegetic time. A common technique is to dissolve (or simply cut) out of a close-up of a thoughtful looking actor into the flashback. In *Ocean's Eleven* (Steven Soderbergh, USA, 2001), a push-in on Tess (Julia Roberts) is dissolved into a golden flashback, lit in hazy orange, as she realises that Danny (George Clooney) has dropped a mobile phone into her pocket.

Create relationships in action

Within a single scene, it is important to connect actions together for storytelling purposes.

Focus film: An eyeline shot like the one shown in **Worksheet 12.4** is a good example. Another important technique is crosscutting to create a relationship between two locations. The whole *Die Hard 3* robbery scene makes extensive use of cross-cutting. One group of robbers are entering the bank from above, the other from below, and by cutting between them, we are made to understand that they are approaching each other. Note also the film grammar of this sequence. Simon's group move predominantly screen L to screen R; Katya, Targo and the drilling machines move predominantly screen R to screen L.

Identify and maintain spatial relationships

The audience needs a confident sense of where they are and where things within the *mise en scène* stand in relation to each other. Techniques such as the master angle, which opens the sequence and is returned to at intervals help with this.

Focus film: The high, wide angle inside the bank at the start of the *Die Hard 3* sequence shows us exactly where all the characters are, and that the building is all but deserted.

Sustain continuity

Bordwell and Thompson describe the approach to filmmaking invented under the vertically integrated Hollywood studios as 'the continuity system'. Continuity editing is devoted to avoiding the jump cut: that is, any edit that the audience actually notices. Consequently, it is also known as 'invisible editing'. This is achieved by following various 'rules', such as:

- The 180 degree rule: You should never cut from one side of an imaginary 180 degree line to the other, as this creates confusion about screen direction. The best explanation of this rule is that football matches are always filmed from only one side of the pitch because otherwise it would look to the viewer as if the teams kept switching ends.

- The 30 degree rule: If cutting between shots on the same figure, the camera must move by more than 30 degrees, or the shot length must be significantly changed. For example, a medium shot on an actor cannot be followed by a medium close up at the same angle or one less than 30 degrees away from it; otherwise the actor would appear to jump towards the spectator.

The rules can be broken, and sometimes are. Students should be able to recognise purposeful jump cuts when they are used. Arthouse films often deliberately use jump cuts to show that they are rejecting Hollywood conventions. *Bloody Sunday* includes many such edits because Greengrass wanted to create the impression of real-life news or documentary footage rather than a smoothly manufactured product. However, we also see jump cuts in expensive Hollywood movies. See **Student notes: Use of jump cuts** at www.bfi.co.uk/tfms. (Enter user name: **filmlang@bfi.org.uk** and password: **te1306fl**.)

Identify important lapses of time; conceal unimportant ones

When we cut to a new location, we require signals to tell us whether or not we are seeing continuous or discontinuous events. Editing can point up those moments in a film when there is a significant shift in time. Usually this would be achieved through contrasts, such as daylight followed by night, a change of location, the introduction of a time code, the introduction of a different musical theme, a long take on the establishing shot at the beginning of the new location, or on the closing shot at the end of the old location.

Film editing always chops out unnecessary chunks of time, in ways that the audience never notices. Imagine a film in which a woman reporter is approached at her desk by her editor, Dan. 'My office, Lois. Now!' he says. He walks out of frame, she looks nervous. Scene cuts to the interior of the editor's office. She is standing, facing the camera; he is seated. We look over his shoulder at her.

In this sequence, the audience neither notice nor care that we did not see Lois stand up and walk into Dan's office. This sort of ellipsis happens all the time in film editing. Its purpose is to control the pace of the scene. If we had wanted to show Lois's nervousness, and build up tension as she approached her interview with Dan, then the editor might have left in the footage of her walk to his office.

Less obviously, ellipsis can be used to take out smaller chunks of movement in order to maintain smoothness of action. For example, say that at the end of his meeting with Lois, Dan gets up from his desk, crosses the office and opens the door to show her out. During this movement, two cuts occur. First we go from an MCU of Dan (looking from Lois's point of view) to an MLS of the two characters, showing him walk past her to the door, and her turning around to follow him. Next we return to her point of view: an MS of his upper body, showing him opening the door for her. If the cuts were made precisely and there was no ellipsis, the edit would not work. In fact the audience would most likely have the impression that Dan was jumping backwards in time. Consequently at each cut, a few seconds of movement will be taken out, effectively jumping forwards in time, and again the audience will not notice.

Having understood the basic functions of editing, students can be encouraged to consider the art of the editor:

- Rhythm and pace

How do the frequency and timing of cuts fit the mood and purposes of the scene?

How are editing and sound integrated?

- Juxtaposition

Editing is the placing of one thing next to another in time. Do the images juxtaposed contrast or complement each other? Are there graphic matches?

Other elements of editing include:

Special effects

The massive development in special effects during recent years has been a particularly important aspect of Hollywood production. The main techniques to be aware of are:

- CGI – computer-generated images, used to create otherwise impossible sequences, such as the huge battles in *The Lord of the Rings: The Two Towers* (Peter Jackson, USA/NZ/Germany, 2002).

- Wire work – a technique developed in Hong Kong martial arts films, allowing for the presentation of massive acrobatic feats, for example, many of those we see in *Spider-Man 2*. Usually combined with chroma key.

- Chroma key – the action is filmed against a blue or green screen, so that the background can be added afterwards. See the DVD extras for either *Spider-Man 2* or *Mission: Impossible 2* (John Woo, USA/Germany, 2000).

- Stunts – physically accomplished, often using stunt doubles, during filming. Students can have great fun watching out for the stunt artists replacing Edward Furlong and Arnold Schwarzenegger in *Terminator 2* (James Cameron, France/USA, 1991).

- Pyrotechnics – fireworks, again mostly done on set, but increasingly it is possible to create, or at least enhance, explosions and fires using CGI. Since this is one of the most dangerous elements of filming, it is likely that CGI will be used increasingly for these scenes.

Sound and sound editing

Again, it is useful to begin by classifying sound into different types. The following four categories can be used to describe all the types of sound we are likely to encounter during a film:

1. Diegetic sound
This arises directly from the world of the story. Its source may be on or off screen. A character on screen speaks, we hear words; a gun is fired in the next room, we hear a bang; horses are approaching, we hear hooves; a radio is playing, we hear music.

2. Non-diegetic sound
We hear this, but it is not produced by anything in the world of the story. The two commonest forms of non-diegetic sound are musical score and voiceover.

3. Synchronous sound
This is diegetic sound produced in the scene we are currently viewing – ie it is synchronised in time with the visuals. It may come from an onscreen source or an off-screen source, but it is within realistic hearing range.

4. Asynchronous sound
This is any sound not produced by the scene we are watching – ie it is not synchronised in time with the visuals. All non-diegetic sound is asynchronous. Some diegetic sound is also asynchronous. In *Ocean's Eleven*, for example, there is a sequence in which Rusty Ryan (Brad Pitt) gives instructions to Terry Benedict (Andy Garcia) as to how some bags are to be taken out of his casino. As we hear Ryan give these instructions, we see – effectively in the future – the bags being carried to the casino doors and loaded into a van. The source of the sound is diegetic, but there is no way we could in reality be seeing and hearing these events simultaneously.

In that scene, asynchronous diegetic sound was used to increase the pace of the action and to clarify some quite complex exposition. There are two other common uses for asynchronous diegetic sound:

- Bridging a cut – we hear the next scene moments before we see it in order to prevent the transition from jarring. This is called a sound bridge.

- Creating a meaningful (possibly ironic) juxtaposition – as in the sequence towards the end of *The Godfather* (Francis Ford Coppola, USA, 1972) where we listen to Michael Corleone at his nephew's christening service while watching a series of murders he has organised.

Sound is manipulated a great deal during post-production. Actors often need to lipsynch (ie perform their lines again in a dubbing studio, matching their onscreen lip movements) because of problems with the original recorded sound. The noise made by onscreen action, which for various technical reasons often cannot be recorded live, has to be created using sound effects libraries and foley artists. Foley is one of the strangest, and most important, jobs in film production. In a room filled with miscellaneous pieces of junk, the foley artist makes sounds by hitting things, shaking things, rubbing things together and so on. These noises are used when constructing the soundscape of the film. Using the documentary on the second *Spider-Man 2* disc, for example, you can show students how the foley artist used a leather flail and some old audio tape to create the sound of Spider-Man's web.

Sometimes, sound is essential to the creation of realism or sense of place. A scene shot in an inland town can be made to seem coastal by the addition of seagull cries. Some sounds need to be emphasised for atmospheric purposes: the creak of a floorboard or the engines of a passing aeroplane, for example.

Focus film: Sometimes, we can hear diegetic sounds with unrealistic clarity. Consider, for example, the bank guard telephoning for help in in the *Die Hard 3* sequence. The audience accepts without question that we can hear the line 'Just relax, mate, and maybe you'll live through this,' which has been processed to give an appropriate telephone line quality. Similarly, in countless Hollywood films, we can hear characters talking inside vehicles at some distance from our point of view. The important thing to remember, and to communicate to students, is that the soundscape, even diegetic sound, is as artificial as everything else.

Frequently, the emotional impact of a sequence is dependent to an enormous degree on the juxtaposition of image and sound, especially soundtrack music. However, because these elements often operate at a subconscious level for the audience, students usually need to be trained to look for them. One very effective strategy is to 'show' sequences without vision (by turning the brightness on the TV to 0, for example) so that only the soundscape is present.

You can then discuss the messages communicated by the various types of sound within the extract. Alternatively, after showing a sequence silently, you can ask the class to suggest what sound they might add to enhance the effect of the visuals on the audience. In this case, it is best to avoid extracts containing much dialogue.

When analysing sound within a film extract, some key questions to ask are:

● Does the music include a recognisable tune or song? What message does this convey in relation to the images?

● Does the music enhance or contradict the meanings suggested by the images?

● Could you describe the music as having a recognisable style (eg a military rhythm)?

● Is the music typical of the film's genre?

● Can you recognise elements of the instrumentation (eg electronic instruments)?

● What tonal range dominates the arrangement (bass, midrange or treble)?

● Are contrasts between sound and silence used?

● How does diegetic background sound increase the audience's sense of realism?

● Is diegetic sound used to increase the effect of any action (emphatic sound)?

● Are there sound bridges or other uses of asynchronous diegetic sound?

● Is there any asynchronous non-diegetic sound, other than music (eg VO)?

● What are the effects of all the above?

Case Studies

Case study 1: Macro analysis – the prison film genre

- Genre
- Narrative
- Representation

The following case study is designed to supply teachers with a clear model for teaching a group of films related by genre. We have chosen a genre that is not commonly studied but which, in our experience, students have enjoyed investigating. The case study and resources can be used as they stand, particularly for example, as an AS unit towards the WJEC AS Level Film Studies FS1 macro analysis, or in providing students with useful examples for work on film genre for OCR A Level Media Studies 2734 unit.

Texts:

- *The Magdalene Sisters* (Peter Mullan, UK, 2002)
- *The Shawshank Redemption* (Frank Darabont, USA, 1994)
- *Birdman of Alcatraz* (John Frankenheimer, USA, 1962)

Viewing notes for these films are available in **Worksheets 14a–c**.

To access worksheets and other online materials go to **www.bfi.org.uk/tfms** and enter User name: **filmlang@bfi.org.uk** and Password: **te1306fl**.

worksheet 14a *The Shawshank Redemption*

Viewing Notes

The Shawshank Redemption (Frank Darabont, USA, 1994) follows Darabont's own script, based on a novella by Stephen King. It may seem to be very much a genre film, competently made, but with very little that is original in its plot and characterisation. On its first cinema release it was not successful, but it became incredibly popular on video, and was eventually voted second greatest movie of all time by users of the Internet Movie Database (www.imbd.com). Among its fans, it inspires a near-religious level of devotion. Part of this may be because the character of Andy Dufresne is presented in the film as a figure of religious inspiration, who teaches his fellow prisoners that the true nature of freedom is within the person.

Stylistically, this is a very old-fashioned film, and not just because of its period setting. Although it was made at a time when Hollywood products were increasingly ironic in their attitudes and approach, this film avoids deliberate cleverness and presents its messages very straight. It could be described as 'folksy' in its tone.

Characterisation and stereotyping
As you watch for the first time, look out for the following genre-typical character types:

- The innocent prisoner
- The rebellious prisoner
- The prisoner who won't give in to anything
- The brutal guard
- The decent guard
- The prison bully
- The corrupt warden
- The institutionalised prisoner

Structure and narrative
You will also see various genre-typical scenes, sequences and plotlines. Be ready for:

- Prisoners tormenting each other to relieve the boredom of prison life;
- A prisoner challenges the system and is thrown into solitary;
- Scenes in the laundry and the canteen;
- A prisoner uses an unusual skill to his advantage;
- An outsider gains the respect of the other prisoners;
- A prisoner learns that education can free him;
- An escape.

© bfi Education 2006

Page 1 of 2   Analysis of Film Language

1 of 2 pages

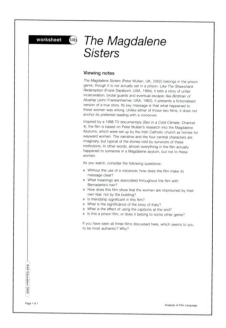

1 of 2 pages

The focus for this genre case study will be *The Magdalene Sisters*, a film that is not as obviously generic as the other two. This should encourage some consideration of the usefulness of genre as an approach to understanding film in general. How can a genre-based reading of this film enhance our understanding of its language?

There are three main reasons *The Magdalene Sisters* is less likely to fit a genre template:

- It is a British film, not the product of a genre-driven Hollywood industry.
- It is an independent film.
- It is a strongly personal project by its writer/director (an auteur film).

None of the above necessarily excludes the possibility that the film will conform to a genre. However, it does suggest that genre will not be among the filmmaker's first considerations. If the film has been shaped by genre, it is because genre structures are a deeper element of film language. Considering its narrative, some possible genres for *The Magdalene Sisters* might be:

a) Convent/monastery film

A very minor genre, but there are a few examples. These films are usually characterised by the central character's struggle for faith and the repression of sexual and romantic desires. *The Nun's Story* (Fred Zinnemann, USA, 1959) and *Black Narcissus* (Michael Powell/Emeric Pressburger, UK, 1947) are famous examples; *The Devils* (Ken Russell, UK, 1971) is perhaps the most extreme. The genre is often combined with others, as it is in the murder mysteries *The Name of the Rose* (Jean-Jacques Annaud, France/Italy/West Germany, 1986) and *Agnes of God* (Norman Jewison, USA, 1985).

The Magdalene Sisters

b) Period drama (subgenre: dark side of the post-war years)

Examples of this subgenre include *Quiz Show* (Robert Redford, USA, 1994), *Stand by Me* (Rob Reiner, USA, 1986) or *Let Him Have It* (Peter Medak, UK, 1991). These films juxtapose a nostalgic and meticulous recreation of the 1950s and early 1960s with harsh and ugly truths about those times. In doing so, they challenge the myth that this was a golden age of innocence and decency.

c) Prison film

This genre has been a staple of film production since the likes of *I am a Fugitive from a Chain Gang* (Mervyn LeRoy, USA, 1939). It has a distinctive generic identity, and includes some significant products of the US industry. *I am a Fugitive from a Chain Gang,* for example, was instrumental in creating Warner Brothers' identity as the 'social commentary' studio in the 1940s.

As context for *The Magdalene Sisters* we will be referring mainly to two other prison films: *Birdman of Alcatraz* and *The Shawshank Redemption*. Through these two films, we can establish all of the main generic and narrative conventions of prison stories. The extent to which *The Magdalene Sisters* conforms to, or deviates from, these conventions should then become clear.

● **Main characteristics of the prison genre**

One reason for the popularity of the prison genre with filmmakers is that it comes with a ready-made set of semiotics. As the French structuralist Michel Foucault explained in his study of the history of imprisonment, *Discipline and Punish*, every element of prison and prison life is designed not merely to have a function, but also to communicate messages to the prisoners and to witnesses. Most of the visual elements of prison films, therefore, can be borrowed directly from reality.

Location and **mise en scène**

Prison films tend, naturally, to take place in prisons. Cells, visiting rooms, warden's offices and corridors tend to be the main spaces in which action takes place. Stone walls, bars, heavy doors, locks, keys, peepholes, uniforms (for prisoners and guards) and weapons are important icons.

It is in the presentation of physical imprisonment that *The Magdalene Sisters* differs most obviously from other prison films. In *The Shawshank Redemption* one of the earliest things we see is an aerial shot, rising over the walls of Shawshank prison. This shot serves a number of purposes, one of which is to establish at the outset the near-impossibility of escape. The walls are so high, and so thick, that nobody could ever get through or over them. This impression is reinforced throughout the film.

By comparison, the Magdalene laundry is barely secure at all. The women are kept imprisoned by society, because there is nowhere else in Ireland for them to go, but mostly by their own feelings of helplessness. As Mullan suggests during his extremely helpful director's commentary on the DVD (at approxmately 46 minutes),

> It was important thematically to suggest that this wasn't Alcatraz, that physical escape wasn't that difficult. It was more the point that you couldn't escape the prison guard of the mind, as it were.

There are several good scenes for discussion in this respect, including the following:

● In chapter 5 of the DVD, at about 29 minutes, Una O'Connor (Mary Murray), who has run away from the convent, is returned to by her father (Peter Mullan).
● In chapter 11, approximately 68 minutes into the film, during sports day, Margaret (Anne-Marie Duff) sneaks off unnoticed during sports day and goes out of the convent garden through an open gate, before coming back in of her own accord.
● In chapter 17, at 100 minutes, Bernadette (Nora-Jane Noone) and Patricia/Rose (Dorothy Duffy) escape from the convent with ridiculous ease, terrorising the sadistic Sister Clementine (Eithne McGuinness) and Sister Jude (Frances Healy) in the process.

Other aspects of the *mise en scène* are more typical of the genre, though usually with a twist on convention.

See **Worksheet 15**.

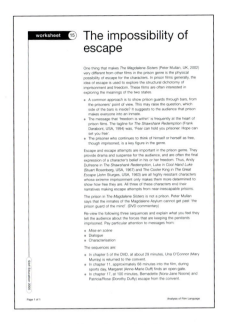

To access worksheets and other online materials go to **www.bfi.org.uk/tfms** and enter User name: **filmlang** and Password: **te1306fl**.

The Magdalene asylum system was centred on laundries, in which the women were forced to work. The laundry in Mullan's film is reminiscent of forced labour scenes generally, which are certainly characteristic of the prison genre. In *The Shawshank Redemption*, we see one group of prisoners tarring a roof and, later, another group are shown digging a road.

The prison laundry is a very common setting, and appears in both *Birdman of Alcatraz* and *The Shawshank Redemption*. The presence of heavy and hot machinery makes laundries useful locations for violence; the transfer of baskets and so on means they can be used for scenes involving contraband; symbolically, the idea of cleansing may reflect a theme of rehabilitation. It is therefore significant that in *The Magdalene Sisters*, Mullan mostly rejects the potential to centre plot, action or symbolism on the laundry. Indeed, after the initial establishment of its existence in the early scenes, it is seldom shown. We could conclude from this that Mullan wishes to diminish the symbolism involved in washing the clothes. This particular form of forced labour was closely identified by the church with the idea of washing away the women's sins; the film sees the whole project as wrong. A lot of screen time devoted to washing clothes might create some unwanted validity for that particular symbolic relationship.

Costume

Uniforms are used in prison movies to define the fundamental opposition between guards and inmates. Often there are quite subtle gradations of costume. In *The Shawshank Redemption*, the evil captain of guards, Byron Hadley (Clancy Brown), wears a uniform with a white shirt, which distinguishes him clearly from the other guards. Prisoners are identified as trustees by slight variations in uniform. The girls' uniforms, in coarse, brown fabric are typical prisoner wear: utilitarian work clothes, designed to emphasise the forced labour aspect of prison life and to reduce the prisoners' sense of individuality. The guards' uniforms in *The Magdalene Sisters* are nuns' habits. To reinforce our understanding that the nuns are primarily functioning as guards, they are seldom shown engaging in religious activity, such as prayer.

See **Worksheet 16**.

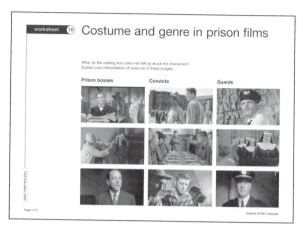

To access worksheets and other online materials go to **www.bfi.org.uk/tfms** and enter User name: **filmlang@bfi.org.uk** and Password: **te1306fl**.

● **Narrative and character**

As Robert McKee and numerous other theorists of film story have proposed, the core of film narrative is conflict. Prison settings naturally generate conflict situations, though in a limited range, which means that the genre can be prone to cliché. Among the commonest conflict scenarios in prison dramas are:

- An innocent prisoner seeks to clear his or her name (conflict with injustice);
- A prisoner is subjected to unwanted sexual attentions (conflict between individuals);
- A prisoner plans and attempts to escape (conflict with the physical world and the system);
- The system tries to break a recalcitrant prisoner (conflict between system and individual);
- A prisoner has to overcome his/her own institutionalisation (conflict with self and system);
- A weak prisoner is bullied (individual conflict with group or other individual);
- A prisoner confronts personal despair and thoughts of suicide (individual conflict with self);
- A prisoner educates him/herself (individual against self, system, expectations of society);
- A good guard stands up to bad guards (individual against individuals or system).

The Shawshank Redemption

The Shawshank Redemption does a remarkable job of including almost all of the above. Only the good guard/bad guard conflict is missing, and *Shawshank*'s writer/director, Frank Darabont, corrected that omission in his next film, *The Green Mile* (USA, 1999).

Prison film plots tend to focus our attention and our sympathy on the prisoners, rather than the guards. Officers are often reduced to stereotypes, and their motivation is seldom explored. Forty-two minutes into *Birdman of Alcatraz*, there is a scene in which the guard, Bull Ransom (Neville Brand) expresses his feelings, but such moments are rare. In the same film, Warden Harvey Shoemaker (Karl Malden) is represented as an honest man, driven by his moral outlook and the desire to rehabilitate, though the film is critical of his methods. *The Shawshank Redemption* simplifies its guards, most of whom are just anonymous men in uniform. Byron Hadley is a sadistic monster; Warden Norton (Bob Gunton) is a corrupt hypocrite. Only once does a guard seem remotely sympathetic: when Wiley (Don McManus) expresses pleasure that Andy Dufresne (Tim Robbins) has obtained some new books for the prison library.

Birdman of Alcatraz

Prisoners also conform to types, but because these characters have more screen time, they tend to develop more depth. Morgan Freeman plays Red, whose role as a dealer in prison contraband at Shawshank is an important aspect of his character, but this only forms one element of a nuanced role. Similarly, in *Birdman of Alcatraz*, Telly Savalas superbly depicts the long process by which Feto Gomez becomes a genre type – the completely institutionalised convict – over a period of many years.

The Magdalene Sisters is completely true to genre with regard to its basic structures of plot and character. The women are unfairly imprisoned. Within the convent, they find themselves exploited economically by the system. They are subjected to physical and sexual abuse and psychological torment. Some, like Bernadette, remain defiant, but learn to work the system; some, like Katy (Britta Smith) are institutionalised. Our attention is focused completely on the inmates; the guards are represented either as monsters or idiots, or in the case of Sister Clementine, as an idiotic monster. The film culminates with an escape sequence.

Narrative techniques

Most films in this genre follow conventional storytelling patterns, though for obvious reasons, the journeys undertaken by the protagonists tend to be psychological and emotional rather than physical. At the centre of all three films is the protagonists' determination to sustain their own individuality in the face of repeated attacks by the system. Where a character's arc in most narratives is developed in response to a concentrated sequence of dramatic events, the prison film depicts a character's reactions to the slow, grinding pressure of many years. This steady process of change could be quite undramatic.

The action in most movies unfolds over a relatively short period of diegetic time. As we saw with *High Noon* (see pp22–38), that period can even be approximately the time the film takes to play. Few films demand the sort of time coding we see in work like *Birdman of Alcatraz* and *The Shawshank Redemption*, in which characters have to live through 19 years of diegesis during about two hours of screen time. Action needs to feel like a smooth process of development, yet we must also be presented with significant periods of ellipsis, with seasons changing, characters' hair turning grey and so on. *The Magdalene Sisters* unfolds over a shorter period of diegesis than the other two films, but still requires signals like the exchange between Margaret and her brother, whom we last saw as a boy, and who has come to rescue her. He is significantly older than the last time we saw him, and she cements our awareness with the line, 'Where the hell have you been for four bloody years?'

A technique that is not used in *The Magdalene Sisters*, but which is leaned on quite heavily by the other two films, is the narrative voiceover (VO). Partly, this technique is used to overcome some of the time coding problems; partly it is used to anchor the film's perspective on events. Many filmmakers dislike VO because they feel it devalues the images, patronises the audience and overemphasises preferred readings. It is often seen as a sign that the direction and/or writing were inadequate. This is a question that can be debated in relation to these two films. Certainly, VO is a technique associated with a more old-fashioned style of filmmaking, and *The Shawshank Redemption* is in many respects a wilfully old-fashioned piece.

Using **Worksheet 17**, students can explore the functions of the narrative VO in key segments of these two films, and experiment with adding a VO to sections of *The Magdalene Sisters*.

To access worksheets and other online materials go to **www.bfi.org.uk/tfms** and enter User name: **filmlang@bfi.org.uk** and Password: **te1306fl**.

● Representation: Themes and symbolism

In all three films, there is a common thematic purpose. They all wish to criticise the idea of incarceration. It is rare to find a film that suggests imprisonment is a good thing, though sometimes, at least, a debate is implied.

Birdman of Alcatraz was a personal project for Burt Lancaster, who saw in the true story of Robert Stroud an opportunity to make a case against the idea that prisons were a useful form of rehabilitation. As the viewing notes point out, the version of Stroud played by Lancaster in the film is highly romanticised, compared with the dangerous, unpredictable and violent man described in other sources.

In the early sections of the film, Stroud is certainly presented as a danger to society. However, his aggressive behaviour is always, at least in part, produced by the conditions of the prison. Once exposed to the power of education, he metamorphoses into a restrained, sensitive man, whose resistance to the prison system has become entirely intellectual.

Stroud's antagonist, Harvey Shoemaker, is a critical figure in this development. Through a level of coincidence that would have been astonishing in real life, his career is interwoven with Stroud's life as a prisoner. First he is warden of Leavenworth, then a representative of the government Bureau of Prisons; finally he becomes warden of Alcatraz. Shoemaker, of course, did not exist: he was invented for the film. This is a metonymic character, designed to stand for the whole philosophy of imprisonment, and with whom Stroud sustains an argument all the way through the story. In a typical exchange, towards the end of the film, the two men discuss their differing ideas about the meaning of the word 'rehabilitate'. Stroud, through his self-education, clearly feels that he has rehabilitated himself; Shoemaker can only see a prisoner refusing to do as he is told. Stroud replies 'That's why you're a failure, Harvey. You and the entire science of penology.'

There is a similar exchange at the end of *The Shawshank Redemption*, during Red's final parole hearing. After nearly 40 years of playing the good con, and trying to meet the expectations of the parole board, Red decides that he has had enough, and is ready to speak his mind on the subject of rehabilitation.

> Not a day goes by I don't feel regret, and not because I'm in here or because you think I should. I look back on myself the way I was...stupid kid who did that terrible crime...wish I could talk sense to him. Tell him how things are. But I can't. That kid's long gone, this old man is all that's left, and I have to live with that. 'Rehabilitated?' That's a bullshit word, so you just go on ahead and stamp that form there, sonny, and stop wasting my damn time. Truth is, I don't give a shit.

These films aim to encourage debate about the ways in which criminals, who may present a danger to society, are dealt with by judicial systems. Thematically, therefore, *The Magdalene Sisters* has a slightly different aim. Although the Garda (Irish police) are shown supporting the Magdalene system by providing security for the parade and helping to retrieve runaways, Mullan has established very clearly in the opening segments that the penitents are not criminals. Here a direct comparison with the prison genre is very illuminating. These young women are shown to be worse off, to have less of a voice and fewer rights, than had they been convicted of a crime. They are not serving time-limited sentences, nor do they have the hope of parole. The issue of rehabilitation, being prepared to re-enter society, is not an issue here. As the character of Katy demonstrates, there is a strong likelihood that the inmates will remain there all their lives.

There is little overt discussion of theme in *The Magdalene Sisters*. Nevertheless, it is far from restrained in its presentation of a point of view regarding the purposes and effects of this form of imprisonment. The final, horrific shot of Crispina (Eileen Walsh) accompanied by a caption stating that she died of anorexia aged 24 in a mental institution does not explicitly condemn the system, but the message is virtually impossible to misread.

Alongside their social issues agenda, prison films tend to develop a range of subsidiary themes, including:

- Hope

  The three films all explore this theme, and its natural opposition – hopelessness. It is connected closely with the themes of freedom and imprisonment. The tagline for *The Shawshank Redemption*, 'Fear can hold you prisoner. Hope can set you free', suggests that freedom and imprisonment are often more states of mind than physical conditions. Andy Dufresne explicitly and repeatedly represents the importance of hope, for example in the scene where he plays Mozart to the prison, and through the slow, tenacious method of his escape. Like *Birdman of Alcatraz*, birds and the open sky are used as symbols of hope at various points within the film, as when Red muses in VO after Andy has escaped:

  > Sometimes it makes me sad, though, Andy being gone. I have to remind myself that some birds aren't meant to be caged, that's all. Their feathers are just too bright...

  During the Alcatraz riot, in *Birdman of* Alcatraz, the old man Stroud, who has maintained his hope through decades of solitary confinement, is explicitly contrasted with a young prisoner who prefers to give up and die, literally of hopelessness, rather than face his future of incarceration. At the end of *The Magdalene Sisters*, Katy's death teaches Bernadette that the intention to be free is all she needs.

- Friendship

  The long diegetic time spans and other conditions unique to the prison setting mean that exploration of same-sex friendship is all but automatically built in to the genre. The central relationship between Red and Andy is critical to *The Shawshank Redemption*; Robert Stroud's friendships with Feto and Bull are carefully constructed in *Birdman of Alcatraz*. *The Magdalene Sisters* presents an environment in which friendships are difficult to form because of the degree of regimentation, and its four women remain quite isolated from each other throughout the film. Only in the final escape sequence is there any real sense of solidarity.

- Identity

  Often a critical theme. The prison is shown attempting to strip prisoners of their sense of self, as in *The Magdalene Sisters* where two of the characters are arbitrarily renamed by Sister Bridget (Geraldine McEwan). Prisoners are identified by numbers, denied the ownership of things that would make them feel individual and are subjected to a regime of enforced institutional behaviour. In these circumstances, the question 'who am I?' often becomes a critical one for characters.

- Masculinity

This is a major theme in *The Shawshank Redemption*, *Birdman of Alcatraz* and many other prison dramas. Perhaps one of the most famous examples is the fistfight between Dragline (George Kennedy) and Luke (Paul Newman) in *Cool Hand Luke (Stuart Rosenberg, USA, 1967)*. As a skinny middle-class intellectual type, Andy Dufresne does not conform to the physical expectations of manliness that dominate the genre. It is interesting to compare his physique to that of Burt Lancaster in *Birdman of Alcatraz*. At the opening of the film, Red bets on Andy being the one who will break down and cry on the first night. He admits that he has been deceived by appearances. An early plot strand, intended to emphasise the idea of masculinity, then follows Andy through a period when he is repeatedly raped by a group of prisoners. A number of prison films represent sex as a factor in the power structure of heterosexual men, for example in *American History X* (Tony Kaye, USA, 1998) when Derek Vineyard (Edward Norton) is raped by the other neo-nazis as punishment for breaking ranks. The key message in *The Shawshank Redemption* is that Andy is never broken by the experience. Though it is designed to diminish his masculinity, it never does so. He continues to fight until circumstances come to his rescue, and the leader of the rapists, Bogs Diamond (Mark Rolston), is beaten so severely by Hadley that he never walks again.

Ultimately, in a macho context designed to emphasise physical violence, both Andy Dufresne and Robert Stroud triumph not through the violence they enact but through the violence they endure. As well as determination, both also demonstrate guile and intelligence, steering the prison situation to their own benefit, and this is presented as a key element of their masculinity, earning the respect of other prisoners and guards.

Expectations surrounding femininity are very different from those surrounding masculinity. This has meant that women's prison dramas, such as *Caged Heat* (Jonathan Demme, USA, 1974), have tended to fall into the exploitation category, full of gratuitous nudity and simplistically coded lesbian characters. *The Magdalene Sisters* is therefore extremely rare as a women's prison film whose intentions are not exploitative. Naturally, it explores the theme of femininity. All the women are effectively being punished for being female, and the structures of the institution are designed to erase their conventional femininity. Sister Bridget's cutting off of Una's hair, and later of Bernadette's, is central to a symbolic structure in the film in which hair stands for femininity. In the orphanage, Bernadette has her hair combed by two adoring younger children; after she escapes, she becomes a trainee hairdresser. In the process of escaping, she threatens Sister Bridget with the scissors. The nuns' habits, of course, are designed to conceal every aspect of their femininity, including their hair.

● Scene comparison

There are numerous genre-typical sequences in these films, which students can compare. Interesting parallels can be explored between the escape sequences in *The Magdalene Sisters* and *The Shawshank Redemption*, for example. Others are listed in **Worksheet 18**.

To access worksheets and other online materials go to **www.bfi.org.uk/tfms** and enter User name: **filmlang@bfi.org.uk** and Password: **te1306fl**.

Case study 2:
Micro analysis of an arthouse movie sequence

- ● Cinematography
- ● *Mise en scène*
- ● Editing
- ● Sound
- ● SFX

Case study text: *Donnie Darko* (Richard Kelly, USA, 2001)

Shot in 28 days on a budget of $4.5 million, Richard Kelly's debut film, *Donnie Darko*, created a buzz when it was first shown at the Sundance Film Festival, and, despite a poor run at the US box office following the 11 September attacks, it has since gained the reputation of a cult film. We feel it is a useful text for studying film language because:

- ● In our experience, A Level students like it. Adolescence is a central theme and they enjoy the enigma it presents.
- ● We think it is important to show how cinematography, *mise en scène*, editing, sound and SFX are used to create film art.
- ● Richard Kelly himself defines a filmmaker as 'a kind of technician or craftsman' (*The Donnie Darko Book*, 2003, x). Since the craft of filmmaking is the focus of this study, it seems an appropriate choice.

Donnie Darko

Before you begin analysing the film with a class, however, it is important to establish what happens. The film is very much open to interpretation and, as we shall see, these interpretations are all linked to film language. A micro analysis is often illuminated by a reading of the whole film and this is particularly true of arthouse films such as *Donnie Darko*. Below we have described four ways of looking at the film, but this is by no means an exhaustive list. Even Kelly's own theory, *The Philosophy of Time Travel*, was written after the event:

> I considered myself to be just a viewer when I wrote it, not the filmmaker. It was meant to be an argument that people could agree or disagree with. Ultimately, I think those pages probably caused people to ask more questions about what it all means. (ibid, xxxii)

● **Interpretation 1: Science-fiction/fantasy**

For Kelly, 'there is no insanity' in the story (DVD commentary). *Donnie Darko* is a science-fiction/fantasy film and can be explained by Roberta Sparrow's *The Philosophy of Time Travel*, written by the director 'to answer all the questions outside of the film' (*The Donnie Darko Book*, xxxii). This is reproduced on the DVD special features and in *The Donnie Darko Book* – both extremely useful resources. In this version, an Artifact (the jet engine) falls from the Primary Universe through the Fourth Dimension in Time into a Tangent Universe. In the film, the events from midnight on 2 October 1988 onwards take place in this Tangent Universe. The Tangent Universe is 'highly unstable, sustaining itself for no longer than several weeks' and, unless the Artifact is returned to the Primary Universe, there is a danger the Tangent Universe 'will collapse in on itself, forming a black hole within the Primary Universe capable of destroying all existence'. Donnie Darko (Jake Gyllenhaal) is the Living Receiver 'chosen to guide the Artifact into its position for its journey back to the Primary Universe'. The Living Receiver is given the powers of a superhero – 'increased strength, telekinesis, mind control, and the ability to conjure fire and water'. The Manipulated Living (the people of Middlesex) and the Manipulated Dead (Frank and Gretchen Ross) assist the Living Receiver in his task. They will do this by using an Ensurance Trap, to undo Frank's and Gretchen Ross's deaths. In Gretchen's words, he has 'to go back in time and take all those hours of darkness and pain and replace them'. Using his superhuman strength, Donnie sends the jet engine through the Time Portal and the Tangent Universe is reversed. Donnie's interpretation of Graham Greene's short story, 'The Destructors' (1954), foreshadows this event: 'Destruction is a form of creation'. At the end, Donnie arrives back in the Primary Universe only moments before the Artifact crashes through his ceiling and kills him (ibid, pp107–119).

● Interpretation 2: Religious

Some fans have suggested Donnie is a Jesus figure who sacrifices himself to save mankind. With the gesture of a miracle worker, for example, Donnie puts his hands on Cherita's head and tells her that everything is going to get better for her. By contrast, Leslie Felperin describes Jim Cunningham (Patrick Swayze), whose initials are JC, as 'a false prophet' ('Darkness Visible', *Sight and Sound*, October 2002) and Donnie himself refers to him as 'the fucking Antichrist'. A sticker inside Seth Devlin's locker reads: 'What would Satan do?' This interpretation of Donnie as the Messiah is acknowledged in 'a sight gag' (*The Donnie Darko Book*, Ii): as Donnie emerges from the Aero theatre, the marquee shows *The Last Temptation of Christ* (Martin Scorsese, USA, 1988). What's more, the film can be explained by the presence of God: Frank, a messenger from God, tells Donnie, 'God loves his children'; according to Dr Monnitoff (Noah Wyle), a wormhole appearing in nature is 'an act of God'; and the possibility of divine intervention is further recognised by Donnie when he whispers to Seth, 'Deus ex machina … Our saviour', a term used in Greek drama. In relation to this, the film also explores the idea of free will and predestination. The liquid spears indicate what Dr Thurman (Katherine Ross) refers to as 'God's master plan'.

● Interpretation 3: Psychological

Indeed, the interpretation of Dr Thurman is also worth considering:

> Donnie's aggressive behaviour, his increased detachment from reality, seem to stem from his inability to cope with the forces in the world that he perceives to be threatening.

She goes onto to describe Donnie as a paranoid schizophrenic who is experiencing 'a daylight hallucination'. Frank, the spears, and the time portal are all figments of his imagination – what psychologists refer to as a coping strategy. In reality, Donnie damages property, commits arson and eventually kills someone. He displaces these aggressive feelings onto his imaginary rabbit, Frank – an allusion to *Harvey* (Henry Koster, USA, 1950). To use Jim Cunningham's words, Frank is 'an anger prisoner' – the repressed id. As we shall see, Donnie constructs this fantasy world, not only from his own experiences, but also his knowledge of popular culture – books, TV and film. But what forces does Donnie find threatening? Authority. Sex. Also, what Peter Bradshaw refers to as 'a kind of thanatos, a yearning for death in the mind of the sufferer' ('Donnie Darko', *The Guardian*, 25 October 2002).

● Interpretation 4: Political

Finally, the film can be read as a political allegory. It ends a week before the 1988 US presidential election and is littered with political references. The opening line of the film is: 'I'm voting for Dukakis'. Similarly, a Ronald Reagan portrait is seen in the reflection of Principal Cole's bookcase when Donnie gets suspended and at the Halloween party someone with a Ronald Reagan mask is jumping up and down on the trampoline – a reference to a Hunter S Thompson photograph. In addition, Ronald Fisher is wearing a Hulk Hogan costume with 'Ronaldmania' written on the shirt. According to Kelly, politics in the film is 'not meant to bash any political party or take any side'. The family, for example, has 'constructive disparity' in its political views which is seen as 'healthy' by the director (DVD commentary). Instead, Kelly is more concerned with what he perceives as a lack of political engagement amongst American teens. As Ms Pomeroy (Drew Barrymore) says to Principal Cole, 'We're losing them to apathy'. Like Donnie, who also wants to 'change things', she is associated visually with the American flag. Setting the film at this point in time highlights the importance of the democratic process and the influence an election can have on the course of history.

To introduce these interpretations to a class, see **Worksheet 19**.

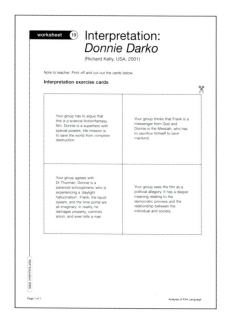

To access worksheets and other online materials go to **www.bfi.org.uk/tfms** and enter User name: **filmlang@bfi.org.uk** and Password: **te1306fl**.

A microanalysis will reveal how cinematography, *mise en scène*, editing, sound and SFX are used to create these meanings in the film.

● Cinematography

According to Steven Poster, the DP, the fact that it was 'a widescreen movie' (ie filmed using an anamorphic lens) allowed Kelly and Poster to compose shots with 'a different canvas' from the one that first time directors normally work with (DVD interview). Indeed, the cinematography in *Donnie Darko* is characterised by its careful composition.

The scene of Donnie and Frank on the golf course, for example, is an example of formal composition – see **Worksheet 20**. Frank is situated at the centre of the screen and facing the camera. Noting that it is a technique often used by Jonathan Demme, Kelly comments:

> What a formal composition does is it forces you into this kind of tunnel vision […] You're forced to look dead centre and it kind of locks the viewer into a certain way of interpreting an image. (DVD commentary)

To access worksheets and other online materials go to **www.bfi.org.uk/tfms** and enter User name: **filmlang@bfi.org.uk** and Password: **te1306fl**.

worksheet 20 Shot composition: *Donnie Darko*
(Richard Kelly, USA, 2001)

It is also a point-of-view shot (the camera is positioned at the same distance that Donnie is from Frank) and the formal composition works to reinforce this point of view, suggesting to the audience that it is an hallucination (Interpretation 3). This technique is repeated in nearly all Donnie's exchanges with Frank.

Another example of composition in *Donnie Darko* is the tracking shot of Donnie walking in front of Jim Cunningham's mansion – see **Worksheet 20**. An image of suburban order is created by the use of horizontal planes – the path, the hedge, the wall, the grass – and these are emphasised by the movement of the camera. The scene is reminiscent of the opening sequence of *Blue Velvet* (David Lynch, USA, 1986). As the sprinklers mysteriously turn off, we cut to a wide shot in which the image is bunched up and the horizontal lines are curved, suggesting a darker world beneath the surface.

● *Mise en scène*

'I guess I found my art among the mundane,' Richard Kelly has said, referring to what he describes as his 'normal' childhood (*The Donnie Darko Book*, ix), and it is through *mise en scène* that he articulates this mundane world – quiet, ordered and beautiful. Indeed, Kelly wanted there to be 'a Norman Rockwell feeling' in the film (ibid, xxxviii). (Norman Rockwell was an illustrator who depicted idealised versions of small-town America.) Lighting is particularly important here. Exterior shots filmed during the day are often lit by a bright sun, as exemplified by Shot 2 on **Worksheet 20**. Green grass and blue sky are common.

For night sequences, Kelly showed his crew Francis Ford Coppola's *Peggy Sue Got Married* (USA, 1986) for its 'idealised nostalgia, its polished, burnished nostalgia' (ibid). Stephen Poster had previously shot *Someone to Watch Over Me* (USA, 1987) for Ridley Scott, a director distinguished for polished cinematography where lighting is key. Paradoxically, the polished look of *Donnie Darko* creates a feeling of hyper-reality, suggesting that all is not what it seems (Interpretation 1). Indeed, the footlights in the Sparkle Motion sequence reference *Lolita*'s school play in Stanley Kubrick's film (USA, 1962), foreshadowing the discovery of Jim Cunningham's 'kiddie porn dungeon' by firemen the next day. This feeling of unreality is more pronounced in the Cunning Visions infomercial, which Poster, who had experience shooting commercials, lit 'so it looks cheesy but still kind of beautiful in its cheesiness' (ibid, xxvi).

The references to *Peggy Sue Got Married* and *Lolita* are also relevant to costume. The glitzy Sparkle Motion costumes are based on the prom dress of Peggy Sue (Kathleen Turner) and the costume Elizabeth Darko (Maggie Gyllenhaal) wears at the Halloween party is modelled on Vivian Darkbloom in *Lolita*. Like Elizabeth, Vivian is the girlfriend of the protagonist's nemesis. As Leslie Felperin points out, 'The name is an anagram of the original novel's author Vladimir Nabokov, the ultimate novelist puppet master, who knew a thing or two about creating characters manipulated by forces they barely comprehend' ('Darkness Visible', *Sight and Sound*, October, 2002).

Costume is very important in the film and the fancy dress party is a fitting climax. People are not what they seem. They are what *The Philosophy of Time Travel* refers to as the Manipulated Living (Interpretation 1) and costume is a way of signifying this disparity between character and role. When Donnie says to Frank, 'Tell me why you're wearing that stupid bunny suit', Frank replies: 'Why are you wearing that stupid man suit?' Nevertheless, Frank's mask, which turns out to be a fancy dress, is suggestive of the death it conceals. Similarly, Donnie's skeleton costume – an allusion to those worn by Johnny and his gang in the fancy dress party in *The Karate Kid* (John G Avildsen, USA, 1984) – foreshadows his own fate. It is also in keeping with his comic book name. As Gretchen Ross notes, his name '[s]ounds like a superhero'.

'I want you to watch the movie screen. I have something I want to show you,' Frank says to Donnie in the cinema, and, as readers of *Donnie Darko*, we would do well to take his advice, as meaning is created through these visual references. Of course, this process is reliant on the audience being 'educated' in film history – in particular, that of the 1980s. This is one difference between an arthouse film and a mainstream film such as *Spider-Man 2* – the way in which the audience are expected to create meaning. To explore this use of intertextuality, see **Worksheet 21**. Other visual motifs to look out for in the film include images of animals (rabbits, dogs, birds, deer) and images of flying (planes, trampolines, angels, birds). These two image schemes are brought together in a shot of Cherita brooding under the Middlesex Mongrel. During her dance, 'Autumn Angel', performed against a backdrop of flying geese, she is temporarily allowed to forget the way other people see her – in terms of her weight. When this illusion is punctured at the end by the unfriendly audience, however, her image of herself reasserts itself. The bronze statue becomes a projection of these feelings.

worksheet 21 **Visual references in *Donnie Darko***
(Richard Kelly, USA, 2001)

To access worksheets and other online materials go to **www.bfi.org.uk/tfms** and enter User name: **filmlang@bfi.org.uk** and Password: **te1306fl**.

The Middlesex Mongrel, Frank's mask, the Infant Memory Generator and other drawings were all created by Kelly, highlighting both his talent as an artist and the importance of *mise en scène* in the film.

● **Editing**

According to Kelly:

> Editing was like playing a game of Jenga only with porcelain blocks and no beer. [...] If you pulled this therapist scene, or that school scene, the plot would have fallen to pieces. (*The Donnie Darko Book*, xliii).

But as Leslie Felperin comments, 'It's infinitely to the film's benefit that Kelly decided to create a more enigmatic edit – possibly guided by the hand of God, or just a wise producer or editor' ('Darkness Visible', *Sight and Sound*, October 2002). The deleted scenes on the DVD emphasise the science-fiction/fantasy elements (Interpretation 1) rather than leaving it open to interpretation.

The editing out of footage can also be used to create effects within a scene. For example, Kelly originally shot footage of Donnie telling Kitty Farmer 'to forcibly insert the exercise card into [her] anus', but in the editing room he realised the comic effect would be greater if he cut straight to the Principal's office:

> You're left wondering what he said, milking the joke for longer. When Kitty repeats it back in front of the parents and the dad laughs, it became three times funnier than it would have been if you saw Donnie tell her to her face. In the end everything comes back to creating suspense. Even comedy is about creating suspense for the punch line. (*The Donnie Darko Book*, xliii)

This is an example of narrative ellipsis – the editing out of plot material.

In addition, a variety of editing effects are used to explore the idea of time in the film. In keeping with Interpretation 1, they demonstrate the malleability of time. At the end, for example, the Tangent Universe unravelling is expressed through a montage of shots that takes us back through the film. Time-lapse photography is used to show the relative speed of this process and reverse motion shots are used to reinforce its backwards direction. The image of the flames retreating along the sofa is particularly poignant. Similarly, when Kelly speeds up footage in a scene, it gives a sense that characters are being propelled along 'a set path' (also Interpretation 1). On the other hand, the use of slow and fast motion emphasises that we are seeing the world from Donnie's point of view (Interpretation 3). Time is subjective, it speeds up and slows down depending on individual experience, and the film seeks to represent this.

Other significant editing techniques used in the film are crosscutting – between the Sparkle Motion performance and Jim Cunningham's mansion. This only becomes significant in retrospect when 'a kiddie porn dungeon' is found in his basement. Also, the use of dissolves during Donnie's encounter with Frank on the golf course creates a dream-like quality to the scene, emphasising again that it is an hallucination (Interpretation 3). See **Worksheet 20**.

● **Sound**

According to Kelly, the soundtrack of a film is critical:

> When a song is used in film – I'm thinking of *Pulp Fiction* or *Goodfellas* or *Boogie Nights* – you can see a film come to life in a new way. The images and music work together like a great tango and it is really magical. (ibid, xxvii)

The music in *Donnie Darko*, for example, is used as a counterpoint to the rest of the film:

> I figured there were opportunities in this story to put a musical code on the character's experience within this era. Picking those songs was, on our part, not to do with making it campy and mocking of the 1980s. The film was mocking that period, so we did not want the music to mock it as well. We wanted the music to be sincere. (ibid)

'Never Tear Us Apart' by INXS, 'Head over Heels' by Tears for Fears and 'West End Girls' by The Pet Shop Boys were already written into the script. 'Never Tear Us Apart' was dropped in favour of 'The Killing Moon' by Echo and the Bunnymen in the opening sequence and 'West End Girls' was dropped in favour of 'Notorious' by Duran Duran during the Sparkle Motion sequence for financial reasons. As Kelly says, they were 'careful with all the lyrics of the songs to make sure that they had meaning'. The lyrics of 'Mad World', for example, a cover of a Tears for Fears song by Gary Jules and Michael Andrews, 'couldn't have been more perfect' in 'describing how this kind of story makes you feel' (DVD commentary). See **Worksheet 22**. Now Kelly makes CDs to accompany new scripts and asks people to listen to them when they read it. He also listens to classical music or film scores while writing.

worksheet 22 **Soundtrack: *Donnie Darko***

(Richard Kelly, USA, 2001)

Read the lyrics of 'Mad World', a cover of a Tears for Fears song by Gary Jules and Michael Andrews, used in the final scene of the film. You can find the lyrics on the internet, for example at, http://www.memoriesfade.com/songs/mw.html

Now answer the following questions:

1. Richard Kelly has commented that the words 'couldn't have been more perfect' in 'describing how this kind of story makes you feel' (DVD commentary). In what ways does the song comment on the scene and the film as a whole?
2. Why else is a soundtrack used in a film?

Research task

Below is a list of the other songs used in the film. Find the lyrics on the internet, identify at what point in the film they are used, and show how they are used to comment on the scene or the film in general:

- 'The Killing Moon' by Echo and the Bunnymen
- 'Head over Heels' by Tears for Fears
- 'Notorious' by Duran Duran
- 'Love Will Tear Us Apart' by Joy Division
- 'Under the Milky Way' by The Church

Page 1 of 1   Analysis of Film Language

Recorded over the period of a month and influenced by the scores of Jerry Goldsmith from the 1970s, the score for *Donnie Darko* was composed by Michael Andrews. In the scene in which Donnie confronts Jim Cunningham, Kelly describes it as 'bizarre' and 'industrial', suggesting there are forces at work underneath the surface (ibid). The title of this particular piece of music is 'Manipulated Living' (Interpretation 1). By contrast, the music in the movie scene, for example, is described by Jake Gyllenhaal as 'filled with sadness' but with 'a tinge of hope' (ibid).

It is also worth noting Frank's voiceover during his encounters with Donnie – another example of non-diegetic sound. In Shot 1 on **Worksheet 20**, the volume of Frank's distorted voiceover does not match the distance from the subject, suggesting that it is heard only by Donnie (Interpretation 3).

● SFX

Donnie Darko was publicised at the Sundance Film Festival as being the first film in the competition to use significant digital effects, illustrating how they are becoming affordable to independent filmmakers. Even so, the film is not a special effects movie. It does not use them to wow the audience, but rather as an imaginative exploration of a fantasy world. They are also 'specific to the story' (*The Donnie Darko Book*, xxx). Kelly's rule with digital effects is to 'only use it when absolutely necessary' (ibid, xxxi), but it is also important to see them as images in their own right. Reminiscent of the water tentacle in *The Abyss* (James Cameron, USA, 1989), for example, the liquid spears are surprisingly human in their behaviour:

> There was a specific design to the spears with respect to each character. Each one was meant to have its own personality. Donnie's spear becomes alarmed when it realised that its host can see it. It begins to taunt him up the stairs. For me the whole effect is either really funny or really disturbing. I go crazy thinking what it could imply. (ibid, xxx)

In this way, the liquid spears can be seen as an expression of a character's soul or psyche. They are also described by Kelly, however, as 'expressionistic', 'bold', and 'a stylised reality' (DVD commentary), in keeping with his view of the film as 'a Salvador Dali comic book' (*The Donnie Darko Book*, xxx). Similarly, in *The Philosophy of Time Travel*, one of the key elements of time travel is water and Kelly wanted to 'link it to the water barrier in the bathroom scenes' (ibid, xxxi) (Interpretation 1). Alternatively, they are there 'to illustrate the metaphysical idea of predestination' (ibid), implying that Donnie is guided by God (Interpretation 2). Samantha is wearing a Dorothy outfit from *The Wizard of Oz* (Victor Fleming, USA, 1939) in the scene, implying that the liquid spears are Donnie's own yellow brick road. As he says, 'If God controls time...then all time is pre-decided. Then everything travels along a set path.'

Kelly got the idea while watching the American football commentator John Madden's CBS chalkboard where he draws electronic lines across the screen to illustrate the movements of the player during a replay: 'I thought, "What if there is some John Madden up there in the cosmos who hits the pause button and draws lines telling us where to go?"' (ibid). Significantly, when the liquid spears first appear, Donnie is watching American football, demonstrating how he creates his fantasy world from his experience of popular culture – in this case, TV (Interpretation 3). Indeed, Kelly showed 'nay-sayers' Peter Jackson's

Heavenly Creatures (Peter Jackson, New Zealand, 1994) in which 'you saw digital effects that came from the character's dementia' (ibid, xxx), reinforcing this psychological interpretation.

In terms of production, Kelly also describes how the liquid spears were created:

> The actors wore those little lights attached to their chests. The liquid spears were then tracked to the actors' movements. This became much more complicated when the camera needed to pan or track with an actor (ibid).

As the actors in the latest *Star Wars* trilogy will know, CGI rely on an actor being able to react to invisible action. During the water barrier effect scene, for example, Jake Gyllenhaal had to mime pressing his hand against the mirror. Designed by Richard Kelly's friend, Kelly Carlton, for a mere $5000, it is an example of how little the digital effects cost. Water is also significant in the brief dream sequence of the flooded school. Inspired by a surrealist photograph by Scott Mutter in which a giant escalator descends into the sea, it not only foreshadows the actual event, but also presents the viewer with a disturbing image of apocalypse – see **Worksheet 23**. This is similar to the time portal itself, imagined as a giant tornado, which also suggests the possibility of destruction. The only other significant use of CGI in the film is the digital manipulation of *The Evil Dead* (Sam Raimi, USA, 1981).

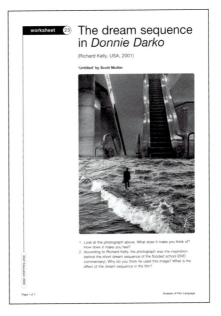

worksheet 23 **The dream sequence in *Donnie Darko***

(Richard Kelly, USA, 2001)

'Untitled' by Scott Mutter

1. Look at the photograph above. What does it make you think of? How does it make you feel?
2. According to Richard Kelly, the photograph was the inspiration behind the short dream sequence of the flooded school (DVD commentary). Why do you think he used this image? What is the effect of the dream sequence in the film?

Page 1 of 1   Analysis of Film Language

To access worksheets and other online materials go to **www.bfi.org.uk/tfms** and enter User name: **filmlang@bfi.org.uk** and Password: **te1306fl**.

● Close textual analysis

Above we have outlined the general features of *Donnie Darko* relating to cinematography, *mise en scène* , editing, sound and SFX. In most Film and Media Studies specifications, however, students are required to complete a close textual analysis, either as coursework or under exam conditions. We have provided two examples below: a shorter analysis that focuses on production – 'Average School Day' – and a longer analysis that can be used as a model answer – 'Cellar Door'.

Sequence 1: Average school day

The scene where Donnie arrives at Middlesex High School references MTV music videos of the 1980s. Kelly recalls seeing the music video for Aerosmith's 'Janie's Got a Gun' (David Fincher, USA, 1989) at the age of 14:

> I saw the video and I thought, 'That person has a vision. That's a movie. I want to see that movie.' That was in the stage of my teens when all I was doing was watching MTV. I had never seen a video that told a story. It was better crafted than most movies I had seen and I was taken aback by it. (ibid, xv)

Significantly, Steven Poster, the DP, had experience shooting such videos. The tone of the sequence, however, is also a homage to what Kelly calls 'the John Hughes version of the eighties' (ibid, l). 'Nothing prepares you for the evil of the world like high school', he comments with reference to his own adolescence (ibid, x), and the scene not only recreates the euphoria of the 1980s pop video, but also the feeling of adolescent disorientation through the use of rolls, whip pans, speed changes, and the 360-degree movement of the camera.

According to Kelly:

> The sequence was originally intended to be a single tracking shot, but the location was so big that it became logistically impossible; as a result we divided it up into four segments. It was choreographed to introduce all the major characters from the school part of the movie, just as we introduced the family earlier in the film with the Echo and the Bunnymen song, and was to be our second 'musical number'. It foreshadows the chain of events, this microcosm of the entire story that is about to unfold. (ibid, xlii)

These 'segments' are described below:

1. The camera rolls upright and dollies left as Donnie and his friends escape the bus and climb the steps of Middlesex High School. The music is 'Head Over Heels' by Tears for Fears.

2. The camera tracks back and forth along the corridor, introducing Seth, Kitty Farmer, Gretchen Ross and Principal Cole. Whip pans are used to mimic the sudden movement of the head when confronted with new characters and fast motion is used to propel characters forward as if along 'a set path'. As we follow Principal Cole outside, overexposure washes out the image with light.

3. The camera tilts down from the Middlesex Mongrel to Cherita before tracking left to arrive, eventually, at a group shot of Jim Cunningham, Kitty Farmer, Principal Cole, Dr Monnitoff and Ms Pomeroy – the 'bad' teachers on the left and the 'good' teachers on the right. We follow Ms Pomeroy and whip pan again to Sparkle Motion practising.

4. A reverse tracking shot takes in Ms Pomeroy walking back inside before panning left as she disappears into her classroom. As we hear the words 'Time flies' from the song, we dissolve to a fast-motion shot of the pupils getting ready for class.

Kelly goes on to describe the production of segment 2 in more detail:

> To efficiently introduce the characters I wanted each actor to be doing something emblematic of their character. The goal was for the audience to understand exactly who these people are without a single line of dialogue. I asked myself, how could we capture the essence of a character in a single moment? Steven Poster pre-rigged the school so that we could have a 360-degree shooting environment. I was hiding with him in one of the classrooms, calling out the camera speed changes to the first AC who along with the Steadicam operator, was the only crewmember in the school hallway. It was a live set; the actors could go anywhere and do anything I wanted them to do. All the slow-motion pieces were created in camera because I don't really care for optical slow motion. It would have been inappropriate for the rhythm of the Tears for Fears song. (ibid, xlii–xliii)

The creation of slow motion 'in camera' involves using a faster camera speed during filming, so when it is played back the movement of the image is slower. This was also true of the fast-motion shot in segment 4, but, in this case, a slower camera speed was used:

> The fast-motion segments were all done optically except for when we fly through the window into Drew's classroom. That one was in camera. I knew it would end with the lyric 'time flies'. My editor Sam Bauer had to cut the song very carefully so that you don't realise that there is about two minutes of it missing. (ibid, xliii)

Overall, the scene is less than three minutes long, but, as we can see, a large amount of time, money and effort was required at each stage of production – pre-production (set design, costume, props, choreography), production (filming, camera speeds, the management of actors), and post-production (editing, sound).

To do a close textual analysis of this scene with a class, use **Worksheet 24**.

To access worksheets and other online materials go to **www.bfi.org.uk/tfms** and enter User name: **filmlang@bfi.org.uk** and Password: **te1306fl**.

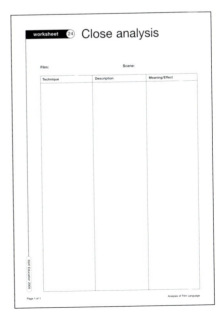

Sequence 2: Cellar Door

'Cellar Door' is, of course, the climax of the film: Gretchen is run over by Frank, Frank's identity is revealed, and Donnie shoots him. The Ensurance Trap is set (Interpretation 1) – Donnie has to go back in time to undo the deaths. But if we are to believe Dr Thurman (Interpretation 3), Donnie cannot undo what has happened – the subsequent time portal sequence is therefore an hallucination or dream that enables him to cope with what he has done.

The scene begins with Donnie, Gretchen, Ronald and Sean cycling to Grandma Death's house. The reference to *ET* (Steven Spielberg, USA, 1982) – bikes and Halloween costumes – creates a nostalgic undertone to the scene. Michael Andrew's haunting score and Steven Poster's lighting add to this. In one shot, for example, we see the cyclists travelling from right to left along a lit horizontal plane in the background. In the foreground, the same lit road curves left. As the camera tracks left, the two join up and the cyclists emerge from one into the other. The curving lines of the road seem to unravel before our eyes – another 'set path' for the characters to follow (Interpretation 1).

At Grandma Death's house, the camera tilts down to reveal the cellar door and pushes in on its subject. We hear Donnie whispering 'Roberta Sparrow' and 'Grandma Death' in a voiceover, as if we are hearing his thoughts. This point of view (Interpretation 3) is reinforced by the formal composition (see Cinematography, p79) and the fact that the camera is the same distance as Donnie is from the subject. The latter is revealed only when we cut away. Donnie's skeleton costume – an allusion to *Karate Kid* (see *Mise en scène, p80*) – foreshadows his own death. Ironically, Gretchen is the only one who isn't wearing a fancy dress, but she is still in disguise. According to Interpretation 1, she is one of the Manipulated Dead. Gretchen isn't even her real name.

We cut to the darkness of the cellar. The low-key lighting creates suspense – a convention of the horror movie. There is no dramatic music, however, only ambient sound. Possibly the sound of birds outside foreshadows the arrival of Roberta Sparrow. To break this silence, Gretchen plays a dramatic chord on the piano, as if she is sending up the conventions of the genre. The camera shakily pushes in on her as she does this – an unsettling moment. In making us aware of conventions of horror, Kelly has lulled us into a false sense of security. It is a red herring. When Gretchen is grabbed from behind, a stab of music – a similarly discordant piano – underscores the action. What began as 'real' diegetic sound becomes 'cinematic' non-diegetic sound, a return to the more conventional mode of storytelling.

As Seth and Ricky drag their victims out of the cellar, the jerky movement of the steadicam and fast editing adds realism and intensity to the violence on screen. Similarly, cutting between Donnie (a high angle shot) and Seth (a low angle shot) reinforces the latter's dominance. As the car approaches Donnie says, 'Deus ex Machina…Our saviour' – ironic as the car will save them, but only after it runs Gretchen over. The red Trans-Am swerves to avoid Roberta Sparrow in the road, hits Gretchen, and skids into the frame – the Phoenix on the hood is a symbol of the new life offered by the final scene. Observant viewers will recognise the car as the one Donnie passes in the opening scene – driven by Frank who has just dropped Elizabeth off. For the rest of us, however, the denouement is still to come.

First of all, the clown's dialogue alerts us to Frank's presence: 'Frank, what did you do?' The clown is a reference to Stephen King's horror novel, *It* (1986), which Rose was reading in the opening sequence. The novel includes a scene in which a character is hit by a car and the passenger gets out dressed like a clown. In keeping with Interpretation 3, it could be argued Donnie is creating an imaginary world out of novels that he too has read.

The subsequent shots lead us to the denouement:

- A low level shot of Frank's legs walking.
- A low level shot of Donnie bending over Gretchen with Frank out of focus in the background. You can just make out the rabbit costume and the mask in his hand.
- A search up shot of Frank resting on the mask.
- A formal composition of Frank in keeping with earlier shots (see Cinematography, p79).

Donnie rises into the frame on a level with his nemesis. As he shoots him, Michael Andrew's atmospheric music suddenly cuts out, as if reality has suddenly impinged on the moment (Interpretation 3), before it starts up again seconds later. The headlamps of the car light the final tableaux: Donnie stares down at Frank, Gretchen behind him on the ground, and Roberta Sparrow, in her white robe, walks slowly away, like a Greek prophet.

As we have seen, *Donnie Darko* uses a variety of cinematic techniques to create film art. In the third case study, we will look at how film language operates in a more mainstream film – *Spider-Man 2*.

Case study 3: Micro analysis of an action movie sequence

Text: *Spider-Man 2* (Sam Raimi, USA, 2004)

Increasingly, students have to perform a textual analysis of decontextualised moving image extracts – an unseen examination. This can be quite an unnerving prospect. In this case study, we provide a detailed account of a three-minute extract from *Spider-Man 2*, referring only to micro, or technical, aspects of film language within the segment itself, avoiding any macro elements or reference to the rest of the film. The only exception to this rule is that we have used character names and those of actors for ease of identification. In a completely unseen analysis of this text, these would not be available.

While the circumstances under which your students have to produce their own analyses may not allow them to achieve this level of detail, it is important that they learn how to construct the closest reading possible: to understand the complexity and richness of film language, and the volume of information that can be extracted from a short sequence.

Spider-Man 2

Working through the sequence can be arranged in a variety of ways. We do not recommend viewing the whole film first, nor should you look at the DVD extras until later in the process. However, once students have worked on the sequence, the documentaries on the second disc will raise their understanding of stunt work and chroma key in this film, as well as editing and sound in Hollywood films generally.

One strategy is to divide a large class into groups, each of which has to focus on a particular aspect of the sequence: group 1 produces notes on *mise en scène*, group 2 works on cinematography and so on. Then reorganise the class so that each new group includes one member from every previous group. They can then assemble their expertise to construct a complete analysis.

From this very detailed reading, you might then ask your students to reduce the material produced in class to, say, 750 words identifying the main patterns and giving key examples. This is excellent preparation for tasks such as the OCR Media Studies unseen close textual analysis. The task can be repeated many times using **Worksheet 24** and further extracts, from this film and others. In this way, students can develop and exercise their critical vocabulary, while also becoming increasingly adept at the interpretation and selection of material.

The sequence begins at the start of chapter 10 on the DVD (21 minutes, 54 seconds into the film) with the opening chords of the song *Hold On* over a rising shot outside Peter Parker's apartment building. It ends with Mary Jane Watson as Cecily in *the Importance of Being Earnest* saying the words 'Yes. I mean no', just over three minutes later.

Worksheet 24 gives students a strategy for constructing a preparatory technical account of any film sequence – for example, while making notes during screenings before an unseen exam. **Worksheet 25** is specifically for a detailed analysis of this sequence, directing students to various key elements.

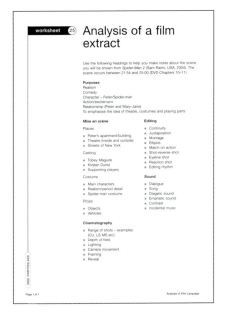

worksheet 25 Analysis of a film extract

Use the following headings to help you make notes about the scene you will be shown from Spider-Man 2 (Sam Raimi, USA, 2004). The scene occurs between 21:54 and 25:00 (DVD Chapters 10–11)

Purposes
Realism
Comedy
Character – Peter/Spider-man
Action/excitement
Relationship (Peter and Mary-Jane)
To emphasise the idea of theatre, costumes and playing parts

Mise en scène

Places
• Peter's apartment/building
• Theatre (inside and outside)
• Streets of New York

Casting
• Tobey Maguire
• Kirsten Dunst
• Supporting players

Costume
• Main characters
• Realism/period detail
• Spider-man costume

Props
• Objects
• Vehicles

Cinematography
• Range of shots – examples (CU, LS MS etc)
• Depth of field
• Lighting
• Camera movement
• Framing
• Reveal

Editing
• Continuity
• Juxtaposition
• Montage
• Ellipsis
• Match on action
• Shot-reverse-shot
• Eyeline shot
• Reaction shot
• Editing rhythm

Sound
• Dialogue
• Song
• Diegetic sound
• Emphatic sound
• Contrast
• Incidental music

©bfi Education 2005

Page 1 of 1   Analysis of Film Language

To access worksheets and other online materials go to **www.bfi.org.uk/tfms** and enter User name: **filmlang@bfi.org.uk** and Password: **te1306fl**.

A technical analysis is only meaningful if it explains the sequence in terms of its communication – in other words, how the techniques used create meaning for the spectator. Consequently, the worksheets ask students to begin by identifying the purposes of the sequence. This may border on the kind of analysis used to examine macro elements, such as genre and narrative, at times, and we should always ask ourselves whether someone who had never seen the film, and perhaps knows nothing whatsoever about Spider-Man as a cultural product, could make the same inferences. You should certainly raise this with students when exploring their responses to the extract.

We have organised this analysis into a sequence of numbered and bulleted notes. In most cases, this is not the way we would expect students to present their finished accounts, but it is useful at the note-making stage to arrange thoughts in this way. It is also natural to do so when analysing a sequence with a class. The webnotes on **Spider-Man 2** contains a finished essay-style presentation of the same material, which can be used as an exemplar for students. See www.bfi.org.uk/tfms.

● **Purposes**

1. To construct believability, the sequence presents a character with unreal powers, but in a realistic context. Spider-Man is juxtaposed with the ordinary. For the most part, the sequence is presented through Hollywood conventions. Compared with a more stylised presentation, such as Tim Burton's *Batman* (USA, 1989) or Ang Lee's *Hulk* (USA, 2003), this extract takes a realist approach.

2. The sequence can be divided into four main segments:

   – It opens with bittersweet comedy, showing Peter Parker as a 'loser' character with no money and perhaps poor self-esteem, but he is more attractive to women (including Mary Jane) than he realises.
   – When Peter escapes death in a random encounter with crime, he reveals his gymnastic powers and amazes two children. Through comedy, he emphasises the difference between his secret identity and the real person.
   – Spider-Man pursues and catches the criminals. A visceral, vertiginous action sequence provides opportunities for big set-piece stunts, CGI and audience excitement. It ends with yet another comic image.
   – Mary Jane feels that Peter has failed her. His duty as a crime-fighter has ruined his romantic project. This is the main narrative purpose of the sequence.

3. The sequence develops a theme of disguise and identity, using a motif of clothing and dressing-up.

● *Mise en scène*

1. Casting is important. Tobey Maguire, although not unattractive, is not a conventionally handsome heroic type. He looks very young, and his face seems to communicate naivety. Audiences are likely to see him as gawky, but intelligent. Physically, his build can seem slight, but, as the 'beefcake' shot at the beginning of the sequence shows, he is actually quite muscular.

2. Kirsten Dunst as Mary Jane is more of a conventional Hollywood beauty. The obvious question created by putting them together is, can romance happen between the 'goofy' boy and the unattainable girl?

3. Supporting players are sketched in, using stereotypes, so as not to distract from the main actors. The ageing Russian landlord, Mr Ditkovitch; his shy, nervous daughter, Ursula, whose interest in Peter is suggested with a look. The florist is just an arm. The ethnicity of the two black children who are amazed by Peter's acrobatics is shorthand for 'streetwise'. The two criminals are thuggish and unshaven.

4. At the start of the sequence, the exterior of Peter's apartment shows how poorly he lives: it is a downbeat, redbrick building, with ancient, flaking paintwork on the windows. The general appearance within is tidy, but run-down, suggesting that he is making the best of his poor circumstances.

5. The interior landing of the building is consistent with the appearance of Peter's apartment, in terms of age and state of repair, maintaining continuity through set design and decoration.

6. The exterior of the theatre is realistically presented. We understand that this is a real play, rather than an amateur production. Also, because of the activity around it, people arriving, we see that the play is quite successful. The sign above the door tells us the play is *The Importance of Being Earnest*, which was the title on Peter's ticket, so it is clear that this is where Peter is going. An image of Mary Jane tells you she is an important actor.

7. Later, when she is on stage, it is essential that a sense of a large, full theatre is created, so that it will be obvious which empty seat is Peter's.

8. We see Mary Jane in a green room. Like Peter, she is preparing herself for the evening, dressing up.

9. The orderly, civilised interior of the theatre, especially since the scene being presented onstage is of upper-class England in the 19th century, contrasts vividly with the chaotic, contemporary American street life outside.

10. A florist's is suggested by a few flower stalls on the street.

11. The streets of New York are located particularly by the presence of yellow cabs among the busy traffic. Extras from a wide variety of ethnic backgrounds create a sense of a busy, lively urban setting. The height of the buildings is an essential aspect of the *mise en scène*, because it will provide opportunities for vertiginous web-swinging.

12. Props are used to construct visual jokes. Peter is shown choosing between two sets of clothes on hangers in his wardrobe: a blue suit and his Spider-Man costume. Later, Peter pays for his flowers and is about to walk off, when the florist takes back all but one of them. Both of these jokes are about Peter's poverty, and lead to the audience wondering if he can afford his love for Mary Jane. Another visual joke is Mr Ditkovitch, finding himself with his trousers down in front of his daughter, which makes him look ridiculous and encourages us to side with Peter over his non-payment of rent.

13. Peter's moped is another comic device, emphasised by his ridiculous helmet. The threatening messages conveyed by the criminals' very powerful car are exaggerated by contrast with the moped, and the latter is actually crushed by the former. We see from this that they are evil men who do not care about the consequences of their actions. Police vehicles (clearly marked NYPD to emphasise location) are shown being defeated by the criminals, and crashing chaotically into each other, suggesting that the forces of law and order are not able to cope. The help of the superhero vigilante is therefore required.

14. Spider-Man's costume is a recognisable icon, highly visible on screen because of its lurid colouring, but also symbolic of the power of the character. Like all superhero costumes, it is tight-fitting, shiny and bright. It also uses two of the colours of the US flag.

15. The guns of the criminals, used to fight against the police and then the unarmed Spider-Man, are an important prop, again signifying power, lawlessness and danger.

● **Cinematography**

1. A rising shot of the exterior (probably a stage) introduces us to the apartment, establishing it clearly through the window. We have a sense of privileged access, as if we are spying on Peter as he dresses.

2. During the preparations part of the sequence, there are many close-ups on Peter. The audience want to see his excitement and nervousness about his evening out. It also increases our understanding that his perspective is the most important one here. The final close-up (reaction shot to Peter's empty chair) on Mary Jane shows us that her disappointment is now the most important aspect of the scene.

3. Two shots in the mirror use selective focus to show us different elements of the *mise en scène* : first Peter, ready to go out, then the ticket with the title of the play readable and a strip of photo-booth pictures of Mary Jane, to ensure that we know how important she is to him.

4. The sequence is set at night, so artificial lighting dominates. However, it is all high key, because the tone of the sequence is basically light-hearted. Very conventional three-point lighting emphasises the main characters and action. Sometimes, the lighting is very dramatic, for example in the overhead shot from the police car about to land on the pedestrians, when all their frightened faces are illuminated. This is, of course, completely unrealistic.

5. In the first part of the sequence there is less camera movement than in the action-driven second half. Such movement as there is during these scenes is very smooth and fluid.

6. By contrast, the car chase shots centred on the criminals include a lot of very wobbly and jerky movement to create a sense of disorganisation and immediacy. These shots, handheld and vehicle-mounted, tend to be confined to the criminals and police.

7. The shots of Spider-Man in action use much smoother camera movement. These look like crane shots. The idea is to communicate Spider-Man's grace, power and control, in contrast with the random, undisciplined criminals he is pursuing.

8. Overhead (bird's eye) shots dramatise the somersault Peter performs over the top of the criminals' car, and a tracking shot around his head is then used to suggest that he is assembling his powers and assessing the situation. This

shot ends by pulling focus on the boy who asks him 'How'd you do that?' The visuals therefore mimic the transference of Peter's attention from his own thoughts to the problem of explaining his powers to the child.

9. Camera movement creates a reveal, when we see an upside-down police car from above, and then the camera cranes down and around to a position where the light will catch the webs suspending the vehicle.

● Editing

Conventional continuity editing dominates in this sequence, which is as a whole constructed to encourage the audience to believe in the impossible.

The major elements of editing are:

1. Establishing shots open each major location;

2. Ellipsis cuts out Peter putting on his shirt;

3. A mixture of shot lengths keeps us orientated and interested;

4. Cross-cutting between Peter's journey and Mary Jane in the theatre builds a relationship between the two points of action;

5. Use of bodies obscuring the screen smoothes the cuts during the first theatre sequence;

6. Match on action during Peter's somersault;

7. Shot-reverse-shot as he speaks to the two boys;

8. Vastly increased number of edits (fast cutting) in the action portion to create dynamism;

9. Longer takes on Spider-Man when swinging, to emphasise the smoothness and scale of this movement; quick cuts when he catches and ties them up to emphasise his speed;

10. Eyeline shot from Mary Jane to Peter's empty seat in the theatre;

11. Massive ellipsis between the time code where an assistant stage manager tells the two actresses there are five minutes to curtain, and the scene on stage. Only about 100 seconds of screen time elapse between these shots. We can assume that most spectators of the film probably do not know that these lines appear in Act 3 of *the Importance of Being Earnest*, but it is certainly obvious that the play is well under way by this point, and Peter is extremely late.

- ## Sound

1. The sequence opens with non-diegetic sound dominant. We hear a song ('Hold On' by Jet) and its lyrics are clearly audible, encouraging us to identify connections with the events onscreen. There are at least two major points of contact here. First, the words 'You forget who you are,' are synchronised with the appearance of the two suits, standing for Peter and Spider-Man; later, the words 'all that you wanted' are heard just as Mary Jane's poster image outside the theatre dominates the screen.

2. The tone of the song is very melancholy, and this undercuts the comic tone of the images, emphasising the sincerity of Peter's character and the true depth of his emotions.

3. At some points, the song is faded down in order to allow snatches of dialogue to be heard. Note that the most important line – Mary Jane's 'You never know who's coming' – is carefully placed during an instrumental fill so that no other words can compromise hers.

4. Mr Ditkovitch, asking for his money, can be heard distinctly, as can his lines in Russian to his daughter, Ursula. These help us to position his character and relationship with Peter. Her conflict – loyalty to her father and attraction to Peter – is communicated silently.

5. The final notes of the song are immediately replaced by diegetic noise – the sounds of the car chase in progress. This signals that the sequence is changing pace and meaning.

6. The flattening of Peter's moped is emphasised by crunching foley work, and then as he somersaults, we hear a whooshing sound effect of movement through air – the diegetic sound is dropped in the mix to emphasise this spectacular action, and remains low during the tracking shot around Peter's head, so that the boy's question cuts through with unrealistic clarity.

7. Asynchronous music reappears on the soundtrack. Now it is sinister, pacy incidental scoring, again, signalling a shift in the action. The diegetic sound is confused and comes from various sources. Traffic and squealing brakes, sirens, gunshots, dialogue. We cannot always connect the sound we hear with its source, and this emphasises the confusion.

8. Crashes are enhanced with diegetic sound – a mixture of foley and sound effects. When a car is smashed up, we can hear the windows and metal being crushed. Like Peter's somersault, when a police car is thrown in the air, its flight is accompanied by a dubbed rushing sound, which stops abruptly as the vehicle is caught and suspended in mid air. In fact, that action is suggested entirely by sound: we do not see it happen.

9. When Spider-Man appears, he is accompanied by a swelling, orchestral theme that suggests his heroism and athletic prowess.

10. His web-shooting makes a somewhat biological squirting sound, carefully judged so as to sound dynamic rather than disgusting.

11. The criminals' yells for help while suspended from the lamppost are audible from an unrealistic distance, but this is necessary to show how Spider-Man has disempowered them.

12. The final musical stab ends the action sequence. The next shot we see is very quiet indeed, emphasising the difference between Peter's world of crime fighting and Mary Jane's civilised, mannered life in the theatre.

13. We can now hear the dialogue of the play, including the ironic question about forgiveness, leading us to wonder whether Mary Jane can forgive Peter.

● Special effects (SFX)

1. There are chroma key sequences combined with stunt work. For example, Peter's somersault over the car, impossible in reality, would have been performed in the studio on wires against a blue screen.

2. There is a great deal of stunt driving during the car-chase sequence, as police vehicles crash into each other in various spectacular ways.

3. Pyrotechnics combine with sound effects to create the appearance of firing and damage from a shotgun and a machine gun.

4. The shots of Spider-Man swooping through the city after the criminals are constructed out of a mixture of wirework, chroma key and CGI. The most spectacular use of CGI occurs when the superhero passes between the cab and trailer of a fast-moving truck at the crossroads. At normal speed, it is impossible to see whether he actually does it; but if you slow the sequence to frame-by-frame, you can see that there are no cheats: he passes through the narrow space in four frames, while the camera waits for the truck to pass. Clearly, this shot could only be achieved through animation.

Having explored this sequence in detail with teacher support, students should feel more confident about approaching other extracts. **Worksheet 25** can continue to be used as a supporting framework for note-making until they feel confident and experienced enough to attempt analysis individually.

Selected glossary

Throughout this guide, we have sought to define technical words and phrases on first use. Where we felt that there was a possibility that a reader dipping into the guide might come across a term and not be able to identify the meaning from context, we have glossed it here for quick reference.

There is, however, a much fuller glossary in the webnotes, which you may wish to print out. We also recommend that you explore the imdb glossary: www.imdb.com/Glossary/, the Yale Film Analysis Guide: http://classes.yale.edu/film-analysis/ and the glossary at www.screenonline.org.uk.

Action code
A signal in the plot that some event will happen – for example, a gallows being prepared signals that a hanging will take place.

Ambient light
Light having the appearance of coming from the sun or moon.

Asynchronous sound
Sound that is produced neither by the action on screen nor within realistic hearing range of the characters.

Audience
The general group of people who are expected to see the film.

Available light
Natural sunlight or artificial light not supplemented by specialised film lighting.

CGI
Computer-generated images – animations and superimposed graphics created with a computer.

Character arc
The development of a character in response to the events in a story.

Cinematography
The process of registering images onto film – includes elements such as framing and lighting.

Continuity
The audience's perception that the film presents a consistent and believable world of cause-and-effect.

Continuity editing
Hollywood conventions for the showing of cause and effect.

Conventions
Elements of plot, character, *mise en scène* and other aspects of film language associated with particular genres and styles. For example, the cut from extreme close up to extreme long shot is a convention of the spaghetti Western. The sophisticated urban setting is a convention of romantic comedy.

Crane shot
Shot taken from a crane-mounted camera.

Cropping
An important element of framing – cropping is the way in which the frame is used to include or exclude aspects of the *mise en scène*.

Crosscutting
Editing device – cutting back and forth between two locations or characters in motion to suggest a relationship between them, eg that one is approaching the other.

Diegesis
The world of the story – for example, diegetic time is time as it is experienced by the characters, rather than the audience.

Dissolve
An edit where one image gradually replaces the other. Sometimes called a cross fade.

Ellipsis
Missing out segments of time – ranging from seconds to years.

Enigma code
A narrative device that creates a mystery so the audience looks for a solution.

Eyeline shot
Shot that reveals what a character in the preceding shot is looking at.

Fast editing
Also called quick cuts or fast cutting – constructing a scene from a large number of short edits.

Foley
The creation of appropriate sounds for onscreen events using a variety of natural sound sources (eg a melon for the stabbing sounds in Hitchcock's *Psycho* (USA, 1960).

Frame
Either the individual images that make up a filmstrip – modern film uses 24 frames per second – or the rectangular shape of the projected image.

Framing
Creating a composed moving image by arranging objects and figures within the frame. Shot length is an important aspect of this.

Genre
A way of organising films into categories, such as Westerns or action movies.

Graphic match
An edit that draws attention to the visual similarity between two scenes.

High concept
Style of Hollywood film characterised by simple plots and expensive action sequences.

High-key lighting
Conventional lighting used for entertainment films: bright and largely free from distracting shadows.

Hollywood studio system
The highly controlled system of film production that operated in Hollywood during the 1930s and 1940s.

Icon/Iconography
Often used interchangeably with symbol/symbolism, an icon is a visual image that has significant meaning within the genre. For example, in Westerns, icons include horses, cactuses, saloon doors and so on.

Jump cut
Any cut that the audience notices. One of the main functions of continuity editing is to avoid jump cuts. Some film styles use jump cuts deliberately.

Juxtaposition
Placing one thing next to another – can occur within a frame (cinematography) or in time (editing).

Kinetic camerawork
Moving the camera around to create a sense of energy and action.

Low-key lighting
Illumination used mostly for noir and horror, with heavy contrast between light and dark.

Macro analysis
Discussion of the larger patterns in a film, such as narrative and genre.

Micro analysis
The analysis of cinematography, *mise en scène*, editing, sound and SFX in a sequence.

Mise en scène
From the French, meaning literally 'put into the scene'. Includes such aspects as location, set, props, costume, make up and lighting.

Non-diegetic sound
Sound not produced by a source within the world of the story – for example, a voiceover or music.

Pre-text
Story events that take place before the beginning of the plot. Also called 'backstory'.

Production
The practical process of planning and making a film.

Pull-out
Pulling a camera back to take in a wider field of vision.

Push-in
Pushing a camera in closer to the subject – not to be confused with a zoom which is a lens movement.

Pyrotechnics
The use of controlled fire and explosions during stunt sequences.

Racking focus/Pulling focus
Shifting the focus from the background to the foreground, or visa versa.

Semiotics
The study of film, or any text, as a system of signs that are read and interpreted by an audience.

SFX
Special effects.

Spectator
An individual member of the audience.

Stab
A sudden burst of music usually used to highlight or create drama in a sequence.

Symbol/Symbolism
An image or sound with a specific meaning that is communicated to the audience. (See **Icon**)

Time code
Anything that signals position in time, eg snow to indicate winter; darkness to suggest night; a clock.

Travelling shot
A tracking shot that follows a subject in motion.

Wipe
An edit in which a vertical line moves horizontally across the screen, pushing one image over the top of another.

References and resources

Bibliography

R Altman, 1999, *Film/Genre*, bfi

J Alton, 1995, *Painting with Light*, University of California Press

D Bordwell and K Thompson, 2004, *Film Art: An Introduction* (7th edition), McGraw Hill

P Bradshaw, 2002, 'Donnie Darko', *The Guardian*, 25 October

J Caughie, 1981, *Theories of Authorship: A Reader*, Routledge

P Cook and M Bernink (eds), 1999, *The Cinema Book* (2nd edition), bfi

J Derrida, 1981, 'The Law of Genre'. In W J T Mitchell (ed), *On Narrative*, University of Chicago Press

P Drummond, 1997, *High Noon*, bfi

L Felperin, 2002, 'Darkness Visible', *Sight and Sound*, October

M Foucault, 1991, *Discipline and Punish: The Birth of the Prison,* Penguin

J Gawelti, 1984, *The Six-Gun Mystique* (2nd edition), Popular Press

R Kelly, 2003, *The Donnie Darko Book*, Faber and Faber

R McKee, 1999, *Story*, Methuen

J Monaco, 2004, *How to Read a Film*, OUP

V Propp, 1969, *Morphology of the Folk Tale*, University of Texas Press

A Thomas, 2004, 'Anatomy of a Blockbuster', *The Guardian*, 11 June

J Vineyard, 2000, *Setting Up Your Shots*, Michael Weise Productions

W Wright, 1975, *Sixguns and Society: A Structural Study of the Western*, University of California Press

Further reading

R Altman (ed), 1992, *Sound Theory/Sound Practice*, Routledge

J Alton, 1995, *Painting in Light*, University of California Press

D Arijon, 1991, *Grammar of the Film Language*, Silman James Press

S Hayward, 2000, *Cinema Studies: The Key Concepts,* Routledge
J Nelmes (ed), 2003, *An Introduction to Film Studies*, Routledge.
P Phillips, 2000, *Understanding Film Texts: Meaning and Experience*, bfi
G Turner, 1999, *Film as Social Practice*, Routledge

Useful websites

http://www.aber.ac.uk/media/Documents/intgenre/intgenre8.html – An
   Introduction to Genre Theory by Daniel Chandler
http://www.bfi.org.uk/education – for further resources including free
   downloadable resources, such as *The Western*
http://www.bfi.org.uk/library – provides useful free study guides for students
http://www.bfi.org.uk/sightandsound – *Sight and Sound* magazine website
http://classes.yale.edu/film-analysis/ – Yale Film Analysis Guide
http:// www.imdb.com – The Internet Movie Database
http://www.imdb.com/Glossary/ – The imdb glossary (provides a huge
   dictionary of filmmaking
http://www.magdalenelaundries.com – Magdalenelaundries.com
http://members.aol.com/Toonsamples/birdman.html – Robert Stroud: The
   Birdman (NOT) of Alcatraz
http://www.prisonexp.org/ – Stanford Prison Experiment slideshow
http:// www.prisonflicks.com – Prison Flicks
http:// www.screenonline.org.uk
http://www.script-o-rama.com – Drew's script-o-rama terminology
http://en.wikipedia.org/wiki/Filming_production_roles – Wikipedia entry on
   film production roles

Selected filmography

Birdman of Alcatraz (John Frankenheimer, USA, 1962)
Die Hard: With a Vengeance (*Die Hard 3*) (John McTiernan, USA, 1995)
Donnie Darko (Richard Kelly, USA, 2001)
High Noon (Fred Zinnemann, USA, 1952)
The Magdalene Sisters (Peter Mullan, UK, 2002)
The Shawshank Redemption (Frank Darabont, USA, 1994)*Spider-Man 2*
   (Sam Raimi, USA, 2004)
Tokyo Story (Yasujiro Ozu, Japan, 1953)

Other resources

Video/DVD

Visions of Light: The Art of Cinematography (Arnold Glassman *et al*, USA, 1992) available from *bfi* Video

Radio

Star Wars: The Original Radio Drama, Penguin Audio Cassette, 1993

Acknowledgements

Once again, thanks to all the students at Gateway Sixth Form College, Leicester, on whom we've guinea pigged our teaching ideas over the years. Especially to those who helped show us what didn't work and what wouldn't work and what couldn't work. You have suffered so that future students won't need to.

Thanks to Vivienne Clark for her ever-tactful support and advice; and to Wendy Earle for trusting us with a tricky project.

Another apology from David to Frances, Ben and Oscar for shameful neglect of family duties during the Easter holidays while getting the first draft of this guide written.

Jeremy would also like to apologise – this time for his strange behaviour in the weeks leading up to the deadline.